YOU WILL NEVER HAVE
FINANCIAL
FREEDOM
BY PAYING OFF YOUR DEBT

CURT WHIPPLE, CSA, CEP

First published by

Financial Freedom Education Institute
Starting Point Publishing
42180 Ford Road, Suite 305
Canton, Michigan 48187
866-PLAN-007

Printing Number
1
First Edition

ISBN 0-9741798-0-9

Additional copies may be available at special discounts for
bulk purchases in the U.S. for church groups, corporations,
institutions, and other organizations. For more information,
please contact: Financial Freedom Education Institute, 47865
Hastings Road, Canton, MI 48188. 877-668-2738

This book is printed on acid-free paper. It meets or exceeds
the guidelines for permanence and durability of the Committee
on Production Guidelines for Book Longevity of the Council on
Library Resources.

DEDICATION

To Connie, Kelly and Kris…the ones I love to be with more than anyone else on earth. Thanks for your love, support and confidence.

To my late friend Gene Taylor. Without whose encouragement this book may have never been written.

Special thanks to Helen Pasakarnis for her time and commitment to editing, Scott Bettinger for his graphics and Keith Craig for bringing it all together.

Table of Contents

INTRODUCTION

The title for this book wasn't very hard to come up with. After all, I was a living example of what so many of us make the mistake of doing with our finances.

For 20 years, I have served in the financial planning and insurance arena. My number one reason for choosing this field was my desire to serve others and help them improve their financial lives. Yet, I was in the same boat as those I was trying so desperately to help. I was constantly broke! I was, as the cliché goes, robbing Peter to pay Paul!

My wife Connie and I began our life together both having great jobs and a terrific income. Connie worked as a secretary to a high-level person in the aerospace industry, and I was a sales manager for a successful radio station. We were your typical yuppies. As soon as we married, we bought our first home in Ontario, California. Then we began to live the good life. We were young and retirement was so far away, it really didn't matter if we saved money or not.

Today Connie is a fabulous cook. However, in the first year of our marriage, there was a definite struggle with cooking. Unless we ate out each night, I would come home to her favorite meal: popcorn and diet soda! I remember one evening she prepared a spaghetti meal. I was so excited! Who cares if the sauce was from a jar? It was better than another bowl of popcorn. We sat down for dinner and I took the bowl of noodles to spoon some onto Connie's plate. The entire bowl of noodles came out in the shape of the bowl....we had popcorn and diet soda that night. Needless to say, we ate dinner out most nights and never brown bagged our lunch during the day. We were interested in one thing...FUN!

About two years into marriage, I began to "mature" and decided we should begin to invest. Did I do it because I wanted to? No way! I did it because we were yuppies and no yuppie would be complete without his or her investment portfolio. I mean after all, what would I talk to the guys on the golf course about if I didn't have some stocks!

I tried the stock market

One day, I saw a commercial of a bull walking through a china shop. It managed to navigate the entire store without knocking down one single piece of china. WOW! That was the company for me! Now I want you to remember, that this was in 1980. The advice was to invest in airline stocks. Well, this was a PROFESSIONAL stockbroker (I would guess his age to be 25) so he must be right. I promptly invested the $3,000 I had managed to tuck away over time. If you research 1980, you'll find out airline stocks were not the place to be. One year later, our $3,000 had shrunk to $1,700! Later I found out that when you walk into a brokerage office with a whopping $3,000, you don't get the top brokers! Imagine that! So, we pulled all of our money out of the market! When did we do this? At the bottom of the market!

I tried real estate

One day I went into the radio station and one of the salesmen was talking about a super deal he had found. He had discovered this great opportunity to buy some land up in a valley north of Los Angeles. Well, stocks didn't work out for me; let's become a real estate tycoon. So I bit!

It was a beautiful March morning in Southern California. Connie and I arrived at the developer's office along with five other couples. The developer was in Orange County and we had a lengthy drive north, so they provided transportation in a small but very comfortable air-conditioned van. Part way up to the property, we stopped for lunch, paid for by the developer. I thought to myself, this is great! I feel so special! I'm an investor!

Finally we arrived. As I looked across the valley, there was nothing! It looked almost dessert-like. I will admit, however, that it did offer some rolling hills. I also remember this one tree standing tall and yet lonely, a fair distance away. I happened to mention to the driver how much I liked trees. I was born and raised in the Midwest where trees were abundant and enhanced any landscape.

Then the developer assigned a driver/salesman and separate car for each of us. Connie and I were driven out to…you guessed it, the piece of land with the lonely tree. We were told how this area was about to boom! People from Los Angeles were being forced north into this valley. If we owned land here, as the people came, prices would go sky-high and we would make more money than we could ever dream of. The picture was being painted and I was soaking up every word! Then the hammer dropped. "Mr. Whipple", he said, "We have someone else interested in this very spot on which you are standing. I would love to see you and your wife get this property and be the ones owning this great view (yeah right)". I wanted the only land around with the tree! On the way back in the van, the sales pitch continued. If you became a landowner, the developer would provide an accountant to do your tax returns, absolutely FREE! Wow! This just kept getting better and better.

Did we buy the land with the lonely tree? You bet we did! After all, we didn't even have to pay for our tax return! Plop! There went another $3,500 down for the lonely tree! It was $3,500 that we had scrimped and saved for (after all of our fun of course) a long time.

About a month later, Tim, the salesman at the radio station (yes, he bought land too) walked in with a long face. He had been by the developer's office and the doors were locked. I quickly began to feel sick again. It was like watching my airline stocks drop, only worse. We both hopped in the car and went directly to the developer's office….or what use to be the office. GONE! No chairs! No reception desk! No phones! Nothing! We were taken!

True to their word, they did do our tax return that year. Two years later though, we received an audit on that same return and ended up paying out more in taxes and penalties.

I experienced the pain of debt first hand

I remember it as if it were yesterday. Connie and I moved to St. Louis, Missouri in 1981. We had made a great profit on our home in Southern California and we were looking for a new home to raise our family. Connie was pregnant with our first child, Kelly Marie. So the home was critical.

I had taken the position of general manager of a radio station in the St. Louis market. It was very unusual to be 27 and a manager in a top-20-radio market. However, I did my ultimate sales job and convinced the owners I could take their station to the top. The station I came from in Orange County, California was one of the top ranked stations so they hired me to hopefully bring some of that success to their station. They really had nothing to lose; the station was ranked 42 out of 42 stations in the ratings.

The owners promised me all I could hope for. Everything the station earned over its current cash flow, I would receive a 10% bonus on top of my salary. Being the cocky 27-year-old, I saw this as no problem.

Connie wanted to be a full time mom and I strongly agreed. So, she left her career upon our move. I saw that as no problem because I would have this station rockin' and rollin', in no time at all.

As we searched for our new home, we finally found one that took Connie's breath away. It was her "Dream Home." Later it would become our nightmare! It was more home than we needed and certainly beyond our price range....at least for now. I just knew that in no time at all, our income would be skyrocketing as the station grew in popularity and revenues. So, what did I do? I bought my wife her dream home, based on what I believed we were going to earn, not on my actual salary. (I can hear many of you already saying dumb, dumb, and dumb)

The stations ratings grew well enough; I just couldn't get revenues to follow. I'll spare you the details on the radio station; suffice to say, the income I anticipated never materialized.

The result of debt!

I would come home at night and find my beautiful wife with tears streaming down her face as she hugged our baby girl, Kelly. I still find tears welling up as I write, thinking of the pain she endured because of my ego and mistakes. Because we could not afford the house we bought, we had built up enormous credit card debt. We were so broke, our living room was empty and so was our dining-room. Our kitchen had some furniture and the huge family room just had a love seat and television in it. Besides our own bed and a crib for Kelly, that was it! Each day Connie would receive four to five calls from creditors demanding their money. It was a sad time in our lives. We were married to our home and we were trapped!

Financial problems are one of the top-two reasons marriages end up in divorce. Debt can destroy families, personal health and well-being. Speaking as a husband and father, it can destroy the heart and confidence of any man. It can cause a wife to lose faith in the man she loves. Debt is a killer!

We tried to sell our house. Only in 1982 it wasn't the best time to sell. Interest rates had sky rocketed and no one was looking to buy. Bankruptcy was an option for some, but not for me. I was taught to honor my debts. In 1983, we finally sold the house on Moonglow Drive for $26,000 less than we paid for it two years before.

So why read this book?

In 1982, I decided to move into a career of insurance and financial planning, a career I still work in today. I began my own firm in 1986, and after 21 years in the industry, I've learned the key concepts to truly help people become financially free.

The stock market and real estate market can be two excellent ways to accumulate assets for your financial future. However, there are other options. The key is knowing some important basics followed by some education, some experience and getting to know a professional in each area.

I decided to write this book in an effort to pass on to others what it has taken me more than 20 years to learn on my own. Key principles that, if followed will help anyone on the journey to financial freedom.

If you're tired of all the debt in your life, this book will show you the way to be **FREE of DEBT!** If you're tired of investing and losing everything you've worked so hard for, you're about to **find answers to successful investing**. If you have tried and tried and **just can't seem to save,** this book will show you the way.

You are about to find the answers you've been searching for! The answers to financial freedom!

CHAPTER ONE

UNDERSTANDING DEBT; TO PAY IT OFF OR NOT TO?

Am I saying that you shouldn't be concerned with paying off your debt? Absolutely not! Of course the ultimate is to be debt free and as you read this book, I'll show you how. **THE PROBLEM** is, if all you do is, focus on paying off your debt, the odds of you finding financial freedom will be slim.

Ask yourself; does every wealthy person on this earth walk around with zero debt? Do you think a real estate tycoon has property around the country or world for that matter and owns it all debt free? Not a chance! There are times when debt can be used as leverage and for positive means.

The problem with most of us is, that we have the wrong kind of debt. Our debt comes from need, necessity or just plain greed. I'm talking about the kind of debt that comes from buying far too much house for your income. The debt I'm speaking of is the result of charging purchases knowing we don't have the money to pay off the bill when it comes in. The wrong kind of debt is when you borrow to buy something you really don't need; with money you don't have and buy products you can't afford. **It's debt that we are using our monthly income from our job to pay for.** You ask, "How else do you pay off debt?" Later,

Notes:

_____

_____

_____

_____

I'll show you how to pay off your debt by using some of your income but also by using other people's money.

Let's call it good debt and bad debt. Good debt is when you buy some investment property with the intention of renting it out and receiving a positive cash flow from it. Bad debt is the kind you accumulate by buying non-appreciable assets and items that have no lasting value. Bad debt doesn't return more cash flow to you. It only robs and steals the life right out of you.

Kevin and Rose

In 1994, I had one of my dearest friends in life call my office and ask for an appointment. My first tendency was to believe Kevin was coming in to meet and talk about investing some assets. Kevin had a good job with GMC Truck and was, I felt, probably making a good income. Rose was a registered nurse and working a full-time shift at Children's Hospital as well. They had a lovely home with two young boys and two really big dogs (Golden Retrievers). Parked in front the house was a brand new GMC dually, one-ton crew cab...a BIG truck! In the garage were a couple of snowmobiles and moored on Lake Erie, was a 28-foot boat. Kevin and Rose seemed to be living "the good life." This is not to say Kevin and Rose were rich or wealthy; rather, it appeared that life was good and everything was under control. It seemed as if each time I would call, I would find they had been out having fun with their toys. Unfortunately, the opposite was true.

It was a beautiful fall morning when Kevin arrived. After exchanging our usual greetings and accolades, we sat down to discuss business. Kevin laid out his financial affairs and I was shocked to discover the

Notes:

_____

_____

_____

_____

mountain of debt that lay before me. It took us nearly the entire morning to sift through the papers and come up with a net worth. The problem was Kevin and Rose's net worth turned out to be a negative. They were about $72,000 in the hole! We're talking the bad kind of debt here.

Kevin and Rose had lived up to this point on the philosophy that the important thing in life was to purely and simply have fun! The debts didn't matter. **AS LONG AS THEY COULD AFFORD THE MONTHLY PAYMENT, THEN THE AMOUNT OF DEBT WAS CONTROLLABLE.**

This is one of the greatest mistakes we can make. We fail to understand that no matter how hard we try, things change. Most people hate change. Change is looked at as bad not good. We run through our life saying what does it matter how in debt I am? The key is I can handle the payments. Then change inevitably happens and we are bound by our debts.

You see debt is not usually a short-term obligation. Most debt, especially the bad kind, will follow us for the next 10 to 25 years. When we base today's debt on that length of time, something is guaranteed to change in our life. And that leaves us with the debt we can't afford and little chance of paying it off.

Even though at the current time Kevin and Rose could handle their payments, they were beginning to feel the squeeze. Also, part of the reason why Kevin came to my office was that he knew he had to make a change in his job. He had two pre-school children at home and was traveling too much. Family life was suffering and so was the marriage.

Notes:

_____

_____

_____

_____

However, Kevin was somewhat trapped! How could he find another job with the same income as his current job without the travel?

When I first met Kevin, years before that meeting in 1994, he was a diesel mechanic making $36,000 per year. It was later that he found his position at GMC Truck, as a field service trainer. In his first year with GMC, he earned $112,000. What a jump in pay! This is when the toys really began to accumulate. As I mentioned, while the income and toys were great, Kevin was searching for something that would allow him more time at home.

Eventually, Kevin found the job he was looking for. It was with a mid size company in Detroit called Michigan CAT. It definitely meant a pay cut, but Kevin and Rose somehow worked it out that they could still handle their established monthly payments. However, they knew they needed a plan to work down their debt. That's when Kevin came in to see me. Unfortunately it turned out to be too late.

Things Began to Crumble

We laid out a plan of debt reduction. However, it was harder than they thought to work on reducing the debt. Things started happening that prevented them from really reducing their debt. The refrigerator broke down. The stove and oven were falling apart. The automobiles needed repairs. Then, the worst happened.

In 1996, Kevin and Rose's world began to crumble. Just before Christmas Kevin unexpectedly lost his job at CAT. Now, he not only had a mountain of debt and bills, he was out of work.

Notes:

_____

_____

_____

_____

During this period, Kevin was in constant communication with me, asking what he should do next. Obviously, the first step was to cut up his credit cards. One day Kevin presented me with a box bound by a ribbon. When I opened it, inside were 20 some credit cards cut up into tiny pieces. I still have that box to this day. The next step, was to communicate with and formulate a plan to pay back the creditors. Then it came time to sell all the toys.

The first to go was the GMC truck. This had been his biggest dream and it turned out to be the loss that hurt the most. Then came the sale of their boat. The list continued until all that could be sold, was.

In a desperate search for work, Kevin found a job through a friend. The job was working on some large trucks in a fleet of mobile wash units. His pay was $10 per hour. This worked out to be a about $22,000 per year. Kevin loved working with his friend and was truly grateful for the job. The tough part was going from $112,000 a year to about $70,000 and then finally to $22,000 while trying to manage his debt load. After selling the Truck, boat, snowmobiles and other major toys, were talking about a debt load still surpassing $50,000.

About 9 months later, the pressure was becoming too great. Kevin remembers it oh too well. "The worst part" Kevin said, "was the constant day to day tension. I remember coming home to the pile of bills, paying as low a payment as I could and only the ones at critical stages. The other bills I would just throw away and wait for the next month to see if they were now critical or which creditors hounded us by phone enough that I would send them some money."

Notes:

_____

_____

_____

_____

The Bottom

In mid 1997, Kevin and Rose had reached their lowest point. The balance on their debts was growing faster than they could pay. Both Kevin and Rose had grown extremely bitter toward life. There were no family vacations, no dining out, NO ANYTHING…except the bills.

Rose recalls, "I was ready to put all of Kev's clothes in a hefty bag and toss them on the front porch. I was only holding on until we got rid of some of the debt, and then I was outta here!"

They went to two different credit-counseling agencies and were shocked to discover the agencies wouldn't even touch them. Both agencies said Kevin and Rose weren't making enough money for them to even be able to help. It was at that point, Kevin was too ashamed to come to me, his friend, and admit he had failed. He and Rose went to see a bankruptcy attorney. They were so broke at this point they couldn't afford to pay the attorney. They worked out a deal to pay him $100 per month and began proceeding forward.

The Break!

Kevin and Rose, being people of faith, began to pray like never before for a way out! About a month into the process of filing bankruptcy, Kevin later told me how he just felt like they needed to put the bankruptcy on hold for a few months. He wasn't sure why, he just knew it was the right thing to do.

In March of 1998, the break came. Kevin got a job with the Chrysler Corporation. The pay wasn't what he once made but it took the family back to a level of income where they could once again begin paying

Notes:

_____

_____

_____

_____

toward the huge debts they were carrying. The pay was good enough that they didn't have to file for bankruptcy!

Kevin once again came to see me and we set up a plan to pay off the debt once and for all. Here now is the miracle. The plan was put in place in March 1998. Eighteen months later, in September of 1999, Kevin came by and gave me one of his huge bear hugs. He and Rose were DEBT FREE with only their mortgage left to pay!

How did they do it? In Chapter 3, I will help you understand the differences between assets and liabilities. That chapter will change your way of thinking about money for the rest of your life. There is a definite strategy...a plan to follow to show you how to build a HUGE net-worth while at the same time becoming debt free.

How about You?

Does it seem that the idea of being debt free is only a dream? Have you tried to save money and found that each time you seem to be making headway, you end up being forced to use your savings for problems that come up unexpectedly? Believe me, I understand!

Up to this point, you've SERIOUSLY tried to save several times. You'd put some money in the bank or a mutual fund. You might put a couple of hundred bucks here or a couple of hundred bucks there. Then something seems to happen. Just as soon as you saved up somewhere between $2,000 and $4,000, something comes up that can't be denied and you have to take some money out. You've been doing this for years. You're frustrated because, **you just can't seem to save!** It seems like life is nothing more than debts and more debt.

Notes:

_____

_____

_____

_____

You're not sure how it happened. One minute you're rolling along and everything seems fine. You're making the payments and life is good. As a matter of fact, once you get those last few debts cleared up, then you're going to really start to save some money for your future.

However, as unexpected expenses come up, you don't have anything in savings, so how do you cover the cost? **You charge it!** I mean what else can you do! You have to fix the problem. You'll just have to pay it off over time (sound familiar?).

It all happened so fast you say. In a matter of days, I went from riding high and getting ready to start saving and investing to being in debt so bad it will take me somewhere between 120 and 240 months to payoff and catch up. AND THAT'S JUST TO GET BACK TO EVEN! Here I am again...**I'M BROKE, IN DEBT and don't have a penny in savings!**

Debt can be like gaining or losing weight. When we are comfortable with our weight, it's easier to eat more than we should and the wrong kinds of food. When we gain weight to a point that our clothes don't fit and we become uncomfortable with our weight, then we become determined to go a diet to get back to our "comfort zone" of weight. Our comfort zone of weight may not be our ideal weight based on our height, but nonetheless, we've hit our comfort zone. This is when the diet is forgotten and we again begin to eat improperly.

When our debt is low and manageable, we're comfortable and tend to possibly spend more than we should. When we spend more than we earn and charge too much, we build up more debt than we are comfortable

Notes:

_____

_____

_____

_____

with. So, we tighten our belts and work hard to reduce the level of debt to where we once again feel comfortable. Our comfort zone of debt, like that of our weight, may not be the best position for us to be in. However, we once again feel in control of our finances.

Each of us has a different comfort level with debt. Some people can have $3,000 to $5,000 in debt and feel in control. It's not insurmountable. Some people are OK with $10,000 to $15,000 (though this is hard for me to grasp!). Then again, some people hate any form of debt and it must be at zero! Whatever your comfort level of debt, when you're at that level, it's like your weight being lower and your clothes fit right. Then things happen, problems occur. Cars break down, roofs leak; furnaces explode. Jobs change and we run through our savings.

Once the savings are gone, we see our debt start to climb and we begin to gain weight. When it stretches too big, we tighten our belts and begin to diet again to bring it back to our comfort zone. Meanwhile, we never seem to get around to saving and investing for the future!

The Good News

You can save and invest and make it work! Anyone can! I don't care how much money you earn, what your education level is or what kind of a job you have. YOU CAN BUILD A FORTUNE! The key to building your fortune, are some basic principals that you most likely, have never been taught. Something so simple, yet in my career as a financial planner, I never read about it in any book or heard about it on any television show or infomercial. It is a plan that was learned in the school of hard knocks. A plan self- developed that has proven successful.

Notes:

_____

_____

_____

_____

Your time has come! By reading this book, you are about to begin a journey that will *finally*, provide the path to your financial freedom.

_____

_____

_____

_____

CHAPTER TWO

FOLLOW THE LEADERS

The office phone rang. It was Tuesday morning and my assistant Kathleen said it was a friend of mine. When I answered, it was Tom, a friend I had seen from time to time but not recently. Tom said that he would like to meet over lunch, to discuss some financial issues that were troubling him. He told me lunch was on him! For some reason, the words *free lunch*, just seem to motivate me. So I was happy to accept.

We met on Friday at a local restaurant. Tom and his wife Lisa are two lovely people, both in their early 30's. They are extremely likable people. We had a great lunch and a good time as friends. When we got down to business, they laid out their current financial holdings. They were looking for some reassurance that they were on track for covering college for their three children and establishing a secure retirement for themselves.

After creating a financial statement in my mind and reviewing their current holdings, I could tell they had done a great job to this point. They were virtually debt free (with the exception of their mortgage). They had enough investments that they were well on their way to meeting their goals. They were even talking of diversifying into some real estate investments. I couldn't find much wrong! I made some suggestions on a few minor issues to improve and then asked them why they were so concerned over what they had accomplished to this point.

Notes:

_____

_____

_____

_____

Tom's answer somewhat surprised me. He said, "Well, as we compare ourselves to some others at our age and what they have accomplished, we just felt like we were way behind and blowing it." While I'm not sure their friends were as financially successful as they portrayed themselves to be, Tom and Lisa were motivated in the same direction that the people they chose to associate with were going.

The important note here is that Tom and Lisa chose to associate with successful people who, like themselves, have been pursuing wise use of their money. We, as humans, tend to become, or desire to become, like those we associate with. Some call it environmental conditioning. Others call it "becoming like those you hang with." It is the answer to the question "What motivates us?" We tend to act, think and talk like the people we are surrounded by. So, if we want to be financially free, then we need to learn to associate with people who are on their way to being financially free, or are already there. Unfortunately, the odds are not in our favor.

It is said that only 1% of America's population would be considered rich. Another 4% of America's population is financially independent. That leaves 95% that is less than financially independent. If we want to become financially free, we need to associate with those who already are! Instead, we find ourselves in the 95% group conforming to the same habits and lifestyles of those that surround us. *People tend not to choose their environment; instead, they go along with whatever environment they find themselves in.* 95% of the time, it's the wrong environment financially!

The reason most of us are comfortable and therefore find ourselves here is because we are in the majority. It's that big huge center area in the

Notes:

middle of society that we call "the middle class." Many people in the middle class believe they are better off than middle class, so they are called the "Upper Middle Class." We live by the idea that (and it's human nature) as long as there is someone worse off than me, than it doesn't matter that someone is better off. We settle for average!

Please don't misunderstand. Am I saying that happiness depends on you getting to the level that most would call rich? Absolutely not! As a matter of fact, if you aren't happy where you're at, you won't be happy where you're going.

There is a story of a man who was frustrated with the town where he lived. He found himself very discouraged whenever he would watch the evening news. It seemed like everything he would see and hear about brought about negative emotions. He would listen and almost without exception, there would be stories of another murder each night. He grew tired of hearing about child abuse, adultery, people stealing and an endless list of the worse things life had to offer. Even the weatherman spoke of the next day being mostly cloudy instead of partly sunny.

He decided he would pack up his family and move to another town, he had never been to, but one that was a great place to live. On the way, he came across a man sitting on the side of the road, apparently just enjoying the day. Needing a break, the family stopped and approached the man and asked him if he were familiar with the town to which they were headed. The man replied that he was familiar with the town. So the traveler, eager to hear good news about the town, asked him what the new town was like. The man alongside the road asked "what was the town you have come from like?" "It was horrible", he replied! "The people weren't friendly; jobs were scarce, and there were thieves and

Notes:

_____

_____

_____

_____

robbers and corrupt politicians!" The stranger on the road slowly looked up and said; "I am afraid that is exactly what you will find in the town you are headed to." With that, the traveling man lowered his head and with a little slower step in his walk, continued down the road to more of the same life he had just left.

While associating with people who are financially better off than you is a good idea for financial purposes, again, you will not find your happiness in that. I am also not implying you should disregard friends who aren't financially free. However, it just makes sense that if you want to be financially free, you should make sure you surround yourself (as much as possible) with financially free people or at least those who are on their way. Also, in order to be happy where you are going, you better make sure you are happy where you are.

Happiness isn't always on the other side of the fence

You see, your life is what you determine it will be! It's your choice! Sometimes, we always feel like the grass MUST be greener on the other side. Sometimes changes in your life are in order! However, as a good friend of mine Brad Powell once asked, *"Do you know where the grass is always greener? It's where you water it!"*

Are you so caught up in the problems of your life and what you don't have or have not accomplished, that you forgot the grass requires some water to be green? Sometimes, we are so busy looking for someplace where the grass is greener that we forget to water the grass in our own backyard. You may not have to search in another town, or the other side of the fence, for your happiness! Perhaps you simply need to water the grass where you are.

Notes:

_____

_____

_____

_____

Who Taught You About Money?

That said, I believe it is our responsibility to be wise with our money and to use and invest it in a manner as if we have been entrusted with it. Let's face it; we aren't all born with the intelligence of how to use our money. It is something we must learn. Here's some questions I would like you to answer.

- Where did you learn how to handle money?
- Who taught you?
- What books about finances have you read lately?

For most of us, we learned much of what we do from our parents. Unfortunately few people can recall sitting down with Mom and Dad and being taught how to become financially free. Why? Because Mom and Dad don't know how! Therefore, the subject is avoided.

If Mom and Dad did share with us what they believe we need to learn to be successful, it is often: go to school, get a good job with good benefits and keep your nose to the grindstone. I believe the reason for this is because that is what our grandparents told our parents. Therefore, it's all they know to share with us about financial issues.

No Formal Education On Finances

While I encourage a good education, I am amazed by how many young people will head off to college for a degree that they will never end up using or don't even want. They believe if they have a college degree, it

Notes:

_____

_____

_____

_____

will mean more income (which it most likely would). However, more income is not the key to financial freedom!

I remember the first time I earned $5,000 in one month. I thought I was in great shape financially. However, I still struggled! Why? I still had a problem with learning financial discipline and what to do with the money I earned. Shortly thereafter, I remember the first time I prepared for our tax return and said to Connie, "Do you realize we earned over $100,000 last year!" Connie's reply was "Yeah right! Then where did it all go?"

More Money is Not the Answer to Your Financial Problems!

I have met people who make over $250,000 or more per year and are still financially broke and in debt. Have you ever heard of lottery winners who two to five years after winning are right back to where they were before winning? Why is this? With a $250,000 income or hitting the lottery jackpot of a million dollars or more you would think they would be financially free?

If you don't get an education in how to handle money, how much you earn is meaningless. You must discover "how" to handle and work with money you earn to become financially free.

Getting your financial education from the right people

Are the people who taught you in college financially free? If not, then step #1 is to find some financially successful people and learn to do what they have done. You may be saying; "Well Curt that's great! I would

Notes:

_____

_____

_____

_____

love to associate with the top one to five percent. However, how do you suggest I meet these people? I mean, you don't just walk up and say: "Hi, you're rich and I'd like to be your friend." I think if you did, you'd be in jail or maimed by a bodyguard! I did it by reading books; they can be a warehouse of information. When carefully selected, they can be your guiding light. Let's face it. We all need mentors and guiding lights in every area of our life, spiritually, financially, as parents, spouses and in most every area of life. I use the Bible as my chief guide spiritually. I carefully select books by authors that can be my financial mentors.

The author who has probably changed my way of thinking more than any other is Robert Kiyosaki. I have gained a valuable education on finances and financial planning over the past 21 years. However, I never realized there was something missing until I learned some foundational truths from Robert. He has a website I highly recommend: www.richdad.com. On this web site, you will find a wealth of information on books, games, and tapes that I know will financially enrich your life.

Unfortunately, many of us allow ourselves to grow according to the environment that *happens* to surround us. It began when we were just kids. At school we wanted to dress just like everyone else. We talked and used the same slang as everyone else. If our closest friends went to college, then we wanted to. If not, then we'd just get a job where they got one. Again, it didn't matter if we could do better, as long as there is someone else doing worse than me, I'm OK. We joke about being in debt and the number of credit cards we carry. We use phrases like "This holiday season really put me behind the eight ball." In reality, we're striving to get the OK from our friends by them saying, "Yeah, I know what you mean, I'm in the same boat!" Then we feel OK because we're not alone. What do you think you would feel like if when you started to

Notes:

_____

_____

_____

_____

joke about your debt, your friends looked at you a bit concerned and said; "You have credit card debt? Wow, I couldn't handle that." My guess is you would begin the next day to work on getting rid of your debt!

Often we fail to understand that our most valuable possession is time! How we use it determines more than we realize. Look at the following chart. It indicates how much money you would earn over 40 years. I have included a 3.5% pay raise each year to make the numbers more realistic.

Current Annual Income	40-Year Total
$ 25,000	$2,113,757
$ 35,000	$2,959,260
$ 50,000	$4,227,514
$100,000	$8,455,028

How are you doing? How much of your income have you invested?

Compounding interest can either be your best friend or your worst enemy! Only *YOU* control that decision! It's not your friends, not your family and not your teachers or professors! *YOU* ultimately are the one who decides how to use your income.

Notes:

_____

_____

_____

_____

Compound interest the killer!

Let's say you had a credit card debt of $4,000. Because you're tight on income, you are making the minimum payment each month of two percent of the balance, or $80. It will take you 108.4 months or nine years to pay off that loan, as long as you continue to simply make the minimum payments. To borrow the $4,000 would have actually cost you $8,672. More than double the amount borrowed! Now, if you compound this by having a number of personal loans and credit cards you owe on, you can imagine the black hole that faces you.

Compound interest…one of the wonders of the world!

If you were to invest that same $80 per month for the same 108.4 months at 8%, you would end up with $12,660 at the end of nine years!

Imagine owning some real estate. Let's assume you bought a house with no money down (more about this later). The house had a value of $100,000, and you ended up putting in a total of $1,000 of your own money to paint and fix up some odds and ends before you rented it. Strictly for an example, we'll assume your monthly payment, including taxes, was $1,000 and you rented the home out at $1,050. You have a positive cash flow of $600 per year. To begin, you earn $600 per year on an outlay of $1,000. That is a 60% return on your investment per year, just from cash flow! This doesn't count the build up in equity due to appreciation and debt reduction.

Going back to our earlier illustration based on 108 months or nine years, let's assume we owned this home for the same period of time. At an average appreciation rate of six percent, the house would now be worth

Notes:

_____

_____

_____

_____

$168,948. If you financed it over 30 years, at the end of 108 months, you would owe $92,408. This would leave you with equity of $76,540! Assuming you never raised your monthly rent and therefore only maintained positive cash flow of $50 per month for 108 months, you would have received $5,400 in positive cash flow plus have $76,540 in equity or a total of $81,940 on an investment of just $1,000. Not bad!

Earl Nightingale, one of the men I respect highly, did a taped series called "Lead the Field." I am confident it probably exists as one of the all-time number one sellers. I strongly recommend you get your own copy; it will help you redirect your thinking to a more positive outlook on life. In this taped series, he had one tape called "Conformity/Non-Conformity." I would like to share some of what he said:

"A man walks down a narrow road and yet right in his own job and stretching clear to the horizon are the rich sunlit fields of opportunity. Between him and these fields however, is a tall hedge, which shields them from his view. This hedge is called conformity. Until he breaks through and cuts his way through this thorny barrier, he will never see nor know the joy's of living fully extended."

You can obtain Earl's taped series and many others like it from Nightingale/Conant at: www.nightingale.com

Notes:

_____

_____

_____

_____

Decisions

- Who do I want to be like?
- If I keep doing what I'm doing today, where will I be in five years?
- Do I have a plan?
- Am I getting into debt or out?
- Am I reading the right books?
- Do I think I already know enough?

You must have a vision, a dream! Ask yourself, is what I am doing today going to keep me on track for achieving my dreams and goals? Am I associating with people whom I can learn good financial habits from? Am I chasing more money, or financial freedom? Remember more money is not the key. Chasing more money can bring pain into your life and the life of your family. Chasing financial freedom can provide the opposite. Don't get the two confused!

Notes:

_____

_____

_____

_____

CHAPTER THREE

"THE GAME PLAN"

Plans are important to life. Think of your last vacation. For most of us, we don't just wake up one morning and say, "Let's go," without a plan of where we're going. We usually plan our trips and vacations out in advance.

Recently, our family decided to take a motor home trip. We flew from Detroit to Denver, rented a motor home and then traveled for two weeks up to the Black Hills of South Dakota and over to Yellowstone Park in Wyoming, finally ending up back in Colorado to do some whitewater rafting at the Gorge. It was a great time we'll never forget.

However, it didn't just get laid out the day before we left. First, I had to rent the motor home. Size and comfort were important, and I know they can be gone early. Therefore, I called in January to rent the home in July. Next, we had to lay out where we would go and what we wanted to see. This, of course, we made a family event. We had maps spread all over the place and had our good friend Nate stop by for some guidance. Nate had done quite a bit of trucking throughout the region and gave us some good information of what not to miss.

Then came the job of making reservations at campgrounds for the trip. While sometimes it can be fun to just go until you feel like stopping, in July if you want to make sure you have a place to stay, you'd better have

Notes:

_____

_____

_____

_____

a reservation. Hooray for the Internet! I jumped on, and in about an hour I had every reservation secured along the planned journey.

Well, as if planning the trip itself weren't enough, we then had some days where we would plan the day! I remember one day, we were staying at the KOA campground just outside of Mt Rushmore. We decided to take advantage of their pancake breakfast that morning. Then the kids wanted to do some fishing. Later that morning we drove down Route 244 and 87. What a beautiful drive, that was! We saw a Ram on the side of the road some prairie dogs, elk and buffalo along the way. We stopped at the "Wind Cave National Park" and walked through the caverns and then took the long ride home and made it to Mt. Rushmore for the evening lighting ceremony. Phew! It was our busiest day, but we made it and loved every minute of it. Looking back, vacations can be a lot of work! I 'm sure you have along with me heard the phrase "I need a vacation from my vacation!"

The point is, we usually have a plan for most every part of our life. Some of us have a plan for each morning and getting ready. Others plan their entire day. What time we'll break for lunch, what time we plan to eat dinner. As we work, we think about that night and plan what we want to do with the evening. We are constantly planning. However, when it comes to finances, for some reason, we never seem to take or make the time to plan our futures. Often, we leave it to chance.

Early in my career as a financial planner, I would meet with people seeking advice. One of the first questions I would ask is: at what age would you like to be able to retire: The ensuing response would many times go like this. The husband would look at his wife and say, "I don't know. I've never thought about it before. Honey, what do you think?"

Notes:

_____

_____

_____

_____

She would look back at him and say; "Oh, I don't know, honey. You're the one who knows about the finances." There would be a long period of silence, thought and some mumbling. He would look back at his wife and say; "I'm just not sure. Do you have any thoughts about this?" To which she would shrug her shoulders and pass the buck back to him. This would continue many times for up to five to ten minutes.

Sometimes, I would want to (but never did) stand on top of my chair and shout, "Will somebody please make a decision!" Once I finally got an answer, I would then ask, "If you were at the retirement age you just gave me, how much money in today's dollars would you like to have as an annual income to retire on?" Once again, I would sit patiently as they discussed the question for what seemed like eternity.

Don't get me wrong; this is why they came to me. They needed help in working through these questions. It was my job and I was happy to help. But it did, at times, get frustrating. It's unfortunate, however, how many people plan things in every area of their life, yet never take the time to read, educate or train themselves enough to plan their financial life or retirement.

Begin With the End in Mind

Many people plan backwards. It goes something like this: "OK, we have cards at the Soper's house at 7 pm. First, I want to take Connie out to dinner at Macaroni Grill on 7 Mile in Northville. In order to make it to Larry and Kathy's house by 7pm, we would need to leave the Grill by 6:40 pm. This means we should be at the restaurant by 5:30 pm. That would mean we leave home, counting traffic at that time of day, by 5 pm.

Notes:

_____

_____

_____

_____

I should therefore plan to quit work by 4:30 pm in order to leave myself enough time to freshen up and get ready to go."

Ever done this or something similar? You see? You are already a great planner. The only reason most people avoid the time to plan their finances is because they aren't comfortable with the "lingo," and they don't understand the vehicles they need on the journey.

If I decided that I wanted to or needed to travel from my hometown of Canton, Michigan to my old hometown of Ontario, California, I have several options. I could, of course, drive there. This would take at least three to four days, depending on how hard I wished to push it. Or, if I needed to be there tomorrow, then I would be forced to find other transportation that would get me there faster. Most likely, this would be a jet and it would take me about four hours. If I had time and it was important to me to be relaxed along the journey, I could also consider the train. You see there are always options in *how you take the journey.* That is a decision you must make.

First, you must know where you want to be. Second, you must decide what vehicles you will use to get there. The vehicles you use may be determined by how much time you have to get there.

Now, imagine trying to go from Michigan to California, thinking the best way for you to go is by car. The only problem is, you've never driven a car and don't know the first thing about how to use one. Most likely, you will begin to think of another option. Why? Because you've never been in a car, it makes you nervous and therefore you decide to either hire someone to drive you, or you hire a pilot or train engineer to get you there. The other option is to decide that you will make the time to take

Notes:

_____

_____

_____

_____

drivers training. You will learn how to drive a car and then after some time on the road, your confidence in driving will grow. Now suddenly the trip doesn't look so scary! You have taught yourself enough about cars to be able to drive yourself.

Financial literacy is the same way. The biggest reason we don't spend more time planning our financial futures, is because we don't know how to "drive" the vehicles available to us. Your decision is to depend on someone else to take you where you wish to go (a financial planner, investment counselor, debt counselor or estate planner), or, make the time to gain the knowledge needed to decide for yourself. Now, you are in control of your future! You're in the driver's seat! In later chapters, I will share with you the knowledge you need to get started on your financial journey.

You may be saying, "I'd love to learn to drive myself. I just don't have the time!" I hope you will hear me loud and clear. *Make the time!*

The learning and developing the financial literacy needed to drive yourself is not as hard as you think, nor will it take as long as you think. I know that if you make the time to learn, you will actually get there much faster than if you don't.

You first step must be to start with the right attitude and frame of mind.

Now, don't turn me off here! I'm sure you're sick and tired of hearing or reading about the importance of attitude from just about every area of your life. I know speed-readers, might want to move ahead in the book

Notes:

_____

_____

_____

_____

to see what's next. Please don't do that! I believe you will learn some key points here that are critical to your financial success.

Perhaps you've heard of the 80/20 rule or the Paraeto Principle. This means that 20% of the people at your job do 80% of the work and so forth in most every area of life. However, in financial affairs, I believe it is a little different. I believe 10% of the people save and control 90% of the assets!

What makes the difference? Why do some people just seem to have golden hands? Why does it seem that everything they touch seems to turn to gold? This may sound trite but it's not because they have hands of gold. It's not because they are smarter than you. It's truly because of their attitude! It's not just that they expect to have good things happen to them: it's their overall view of the world and of life.

Look at it this way. Whenever we are struggling financially, it always seems as if there is never enough money. We look down the road and get depressed and frustrated because it seems that for our whole life, no matter how hard we strive, how hard we work, or how much we make, there just never seems to be enough. There is a passage in the Bible that says something like this: "The more you need money, the more it seems to sprout wings and fly away."

Those who seem to never have a problem with money are most likely in that position because *they see a world full of money!* Therefore, solving the problem of money isn't a big deal! It's simply a matter of finding a vehicle that will take them from point "A," where they are, to point "B," where they want to be.

Notes:

_____

_____

_____

_____

When we are struggling financially, we see a world of not enough money. Do you think people who are well off NEVER have financial problems? I'll bet in most cases they do have problems from time to time. However, their problems are short lived. Why? Because they see more money than the mind can imagine and know the answer to their problem is not money.

Let's look at one example in Donald Trump:

The difference between someone like Donald Trump and most people is that he knows enough about all the ways to access the world of money and how to use it. Most people have never made the time to educate themselves on financial literacy and financial vehicles to become comfortable enough to drive them!

Let's look at one example, in Donald Trump. Donald started his adventures in real estate in Cincinnati, Ohio. He was sent there to renovate a large apartment building and eventually sold it for a rather large profit. After his first success was under his belt, he then found his second opportunity in real estate when he was offered to buy the Grand Central Station in New York. After many tries to find a buyer for the property, he finally got a deal with the Hilton Hotel chain. Eventually the Grand Central became the Grand Hyatt Hotel.

Donald got into casinos when he heard a report on radio of a pending strike in Las Vegas. As a result, he noticed that Hilton's stock value dropped 10% on the news. Intrigued as to why a strike impacting just two Hilton Hotels worldwide would cause the stock to drop 10%, he discovered that virtually 90% of the Hilton Hotel chains income came from those two hotels in Las Vegas. Therefore, it was no surprise when

Notes:

_____

_____

_____

_____

suddenly Donald Trump built the Taj-Mahal and Trump Castle casinos in Atlantic City.

By the late 1980's, Donald had built Trump Tower, Trump Parc and more than 24,000 rental and co-op apartments. He also had developed Trump Shuttle Airline and his casino's mentioned above. Just a few years later, in 1990, Donald Trump faced bankruptcy with over two billion in loans due. The bankruptcy took its effect in many ways and eventually Donald and his wife Ivana, ended their marriage.

As bad as things were for Donald Trump, He now, just 12 years later is worth an estimated 1.7 billion dollars.

While I am not in any way saying we should all model Donald Trump, the point is that he did not see his problem as not having enough money. He knew the world was full of money.

The difference between some one like Donald Trump and most people is that he knows enough about all the ways to access the world of money and how to use it. Most people have never made the time to educate themselves in financial literacy and financial vehicles to become comfortable enough to drive them!

How do you learn financial literacy?

First, you must decide you're sick and tired of walking. Enough so, that you're willing to learn how to drive your financial car. It's worth ***"making the time."*** Sure you're nervous, but it's worth the risk. Don't worry about running out of gas because the world is filled with gas. There are gas stations everywhere! You simply must learn how to drive

Notes:

_____

_____

_____

_____

and then learn where to find the gas stations. It's faster to take the time and learn about financial vehicles and reach your goals at the right time, than it is to quickly choose a vehicle without learning about it and never figure out how to start the engine.

Watch Out for the Killers of Dreams!

"Life is either a daring adventure or it's nothing at all." Helen Keller made that statement and I believe in its merit.

One of the greatest obstacles to our financial freedom can be the ones who love and care for us the most: our family and friends. While their intentions are good, they can prevent us from taking the right road. So if they have good intentions, why the roadblocks? There can be two reasons. *First, they don't want to see you get hurt!* They are trying to protect you from any mistakes or pain in life. This is admirable and normal. However, if we are never willing to make a mistake, then we can't ever go anywhere.

Maybe your family members have tried different ways of investing and failed at their first attempt. The idea of losing money is too much to handle for many people. Rather than identify, what they did wrong and try again, they may say, "I'll never do that again". Then they make sure you don't do try it.

Not meaning to overkill an illustration, allow me to go back to the automobile. Driving a car can be risky. We have all heard of traffic accidents that have been fatal at times. So then, why do we drive cars if there is a chance that we could be killed? It's because, we believe it is worth the risk and the odds are in our favor.

Notes:

I'm not sure how many cars are on the road in the United States today. However, with the population closing in on three hundred million, and while not every adult owns a car, there are many who own multiple cars. It wouldn't surprise me if someone said there were over two hundred million cars on the road.

A recent statistic off the Internet shows that there were 6,356,000 car accidents in the United States in the year 2000. Of those accidents, 41,821 were fatal. While I take nothing away from the seriousness of a loss of life in a car accident, if my estimate of cars is correct, only 3% of all cars on the road have an accident during the year. Of the estimated cars in the U.S., that would mean .0002 % result in a fatal accident. That's 2/100th of a percent. So while driving a car can be risky, the odds against a fatal accident are very small.

So many times people receive their training from the wrong source. They may have been at work and heard about the "hot tip" the person in the next cubicle offers. They're told it's no risk, offers the potential to double your money by the end of the year and, oh yeah, it's tax-free too! They know they have to do something because the financial road they are on sure isn't cutting it. The investment is only $2,000. So what the heck: let's do it. Two weeks later they find out the "sure bet" was on its way to going belly up about the time they signed over the check.

I remember a time while living in the St. Louis area when, my best friend at the time, Steve, approached me about a hot tip! The details may not be totally accurate but it went something like this: His brother lived in the South and worked for a company that offered investments in oil drilling sights. There was a new one just being developed and the

Notes:

_____

_____

_____

_____

company was looking for investors. The company had already drilled 14 other wells and struck oil. Therefore there was wealth for all who had invested on each one. This was a sure bet! The company never missed.........until this well. It was dry! Thankfully, I passed on the offer. Steve learned a valuable lesson.

My point is that many people try to invest without training. Then when the results are negative, they deem investing is just too risky for them. They succumb to a life of mediocrity and as little risk as possible. Because your family loves you, they don't want to see you hurt. Therefore, they will do what they can to protect you against the possibilities of pain. What's interesting is that if you go ahead with your financial plan, they may call you crazy. Then when you succeed at your financial plan, they call you a genius, or a person with golden hands, or, believe it or not, you're just lucky! In reality, you simply decided to get an education and training before you set out down the financial highway. You reduced the risk and insured your dream of reaching your destination because you made the time to learn.

Now let's talk about the second reason we are sometimes held back. Ever heard of the saying "misery loves company?" That's the second reason. We could be held back by friends or acquaintances not even close to us. You may have heard about the crab basket theory. It is said that if you put a bunch of crabs in a basket they will never climb out. They have the ability to do so. But each time one of them decides to crawl out, just as they are nearing the top of the basket, one of the other crabs will reach up and pull them back down into the basket.

Notes:

_____

_____

_____

_____

Friends and acquaintances can do the same. If you begin to move to a better position in life financially, it says to them, that they are failing. It's comfortable to stay together, because that means we're all OK.

Dreams and goals are critical to a fulfilled life!

If money were no object, what would you be doing with your life? If you had 10 million dollars in the bank, would you still be working at the same job you are at today? Would you live in the same house and drive the same car? Would you give more to your church or favorite charity? Would you travel to various places around the world? Think about it for just one minute. What would it be like?

Now admit it. Did your pulse quicken just a little bit while reading the last paragraph? Just thinking about what it would be like can be exhilarating! This is what dreams and goals can do for your life. Please remember, more money does not buy you happiness. As mentioned earlier, there are many rich people who are extremely unhappy. If you're not happy where you're at today, you'll find it hard to be happy where you're going. However, the exhilaration and joy that can come from dreams and goals of a better financial future cannot be denied. Life offers so much that can be tied to financial freedom. It's worth taking the time to learn and gain the financial literacy needed to "move on down the road". Want to join me? Read on, and I'll teach you how!

Notes:

_____

_____

_____

_____

CHAPTER FOUR

THE FREEDOM PLAN

"What many people need is not more money. More money X bad habits still = 0 money. People need to learn how to handle the money they have. More money X good financial habits = financial freedom!"

This book is dedicated to helping you reduce and eliminate debt. At the same time you need to be building your net-worth. I believe you should never consider one without doing the other. Some advisors will tell you, that the very first thing you should do is eliminate your debt before ever beginning to save and invest. While it is possible to succeed with this approach, the percentage of those who succeed is very small. They never get to the part about investing for their future, because life is now focused on nothing but debt and more debt. The frustration of their debt ends up killing the dream of financial freedom. The entire premise of this book is that you never try to eliminate your debt without, at the same time, beginning to build your financial net worth.

Some of the Root Causes of Debt

It's every high school or college graduate's dream to leave school and find that perfect job. You know, the one where you get paid a grossly high salary, have four weeks vacation, job security and a pension plan that will take care of you for the rest of your life. Why do most

Notes:

_____

_____

_____

_____

graduates expect this? For the answer, look at where their parents came from.

My parents, who at this writing were both 82 years old, lived their childhood in the great depression of the '30's. They grew up experiencing the financial frustrations of that period of time. Therefore, when they got married, they didn't expect to "start off" with everything the world had to offer. They believed in the American Dream, and that if you work hard, you can have it. But they never expected it to be given to them.

Today, most young adults are beginning life on their own with a different perspective. They grew up in a society where what you want is what you expect to get. They, for the most part, are sometimes under the false impression that what their parents have had ought to be theirs right off the bat. Why not? As soon as they were out of school, they received a mailer from a bank or credit card company offering them all of the credit their parents have. Interest rate? What interest rate? The fliers promise I can buy what ever I want and the payments will only be two percent of what I buy! So, as long as I can handle the payments, what does it matter what the item costs?

Unfortunately, their parents have unintentionally fooled these young adults. The younger set grew up seeing all of the "stuff" that their parents had attained. However, they never really saw the amount or level of work it took to achieve this lifestyle. Nor did they see the debt, stress, pressure and hardships their parent's debt cost, if they did it with borrowing.

Notes:
_____

_____

_____

_____

In the '70's and '80's, the term "keepin' up with the Jones'" never had greater meaning. As our country's wealth began to flourish, many people truly did see tremendous increases in their income. Unfortunately, others did not. In order to not feel left behind, many people began to buy more and more of their purchases on credit. What they were really doing was not only digging a hole they may never be able to climb out of, debt-wise, they were destroying any possibility of one day finding financial freedom. Furthermore, they passed on their idea of how to handle money to their children. The idea of debt has now compounded to figures never before heard of or imagined.

Consider some of the facts:

1. In 1990, the typical U.S. household saved 7.8% of its income. In 1999, the same family spent 0.1% MORE than it earned. (Drowning In Debt, Gary Belsky)

2. In 1992, the average American had debt payments equaling 75% of his household income. In 2001, it was **100%** of household income. (Business Week 8/3/02)

3. A University of Michigan study showed half of low-income families with high consumer debt and low net worth in 1994, were still broke in 1999. The average indebtedness grew from $2,900 to over $18,500. (Newsweek 8/27/01)

4. In 2001, there were 538,000,000,000 credit cards in the United States. (Ashbury Park Press 2/18/02)

Notes:

_____

_____

_____

_____

5. In 2000, total public debt in the U.S. stood at $3,266,222,376,162.12. (www.publicdebt.treas.gov)

6. In June 2001, the interest paid on household debt was $80,607,325,062.44. (www.publicdebt.treas.gov)

7. Only 32% of all parents talk to their kids about money! (NFCC News, 6/20/01)

Today, most people under the age of 45 have been more focused on possessions than on financial freedom. The sad truth is, that if we were to focus first on financial freedom, we could also have the possessions! But when the first and primary focus is on possessions, we will never have financial freedom!

So, today, the American public is in its worst debt crisis in history. Let me ask you a question. Is there a time coming when the economy will punish those in so much debt? I believe the answer is a firm YES! At the writing of this book, we are seeing just the beginning stages of the problem. It will only get worse!

I live in southeastern Michigan, the motor capital of the world. Many autoworkers have been earning more money than they ever dreamed of when they first began their job. Overtime, until recently, was at an all time high. Many tell me they have been working 20 to 40 hours of overtime at an hourly rate called time- and-a-half. Some have even been clearing over $100,000 per year based on the great economy we've enjoyed over the last 20 years. What happens when the overtime stops? What happens when workers who are used to making $100,000 per year (and have now adjusted to it) are suddenly making $60,000 per year?

Notes:

_____

_____

_____

_____

Can they afford to lose more than $3,300 every month? I don't think so. Then, the final question is how do they pay those "easy" monthly payments when 40% of their income disappears?

Never before, has their been a time where teaching people how to be debt-free AND how to build a financial net worth could be more critical. You may be reading and saying to yourself; "I have some debt but I'm not that bad off." I hope you're right! Let's do a quick check to see.

Symptoms of Personal Financial Problems

1. You are preoccupied with thoughts about money
   Let's face it. We all think about money! We all want more of it! What I am saying is that if you are constantly mulling around in your mind how to pay for something you've bought or are about to buy, you probably can't really afford it. However, you want it so badly, you can't stop. It's all you think about.
2. You argue within your family about money matters.
3. You can't or don't pay off your credit cards in full each month.
4. You need or have seriously considered a consolidation/home equity loan.
5. You receive notices of past due accounts.
6. You charge items because you can't pay cash.
7. You use spending as emotional therapy.
8. You spend impulsively.
   It's hard for you to walk away and think about the purchase. I mean, "what if the sale isn't there tomorrow?"
9. You invade savings to meet current monthly expenses.
10. Your net worth does not increase annually.
11. You don't know what "net worth" means.

Notes:

_____

_____

_____

_____

12. You "just can't seem to save!"
13. You are underinsured.
14. You wish you had a plan for investing but you don't.

If any of the above items relate to you, this could represent some financial problems. By the end of this book, I will teach you how to totally change your way of thinking about money! My plan will take you right to the root of the financial problems that may be haunting you and not only help you get rid of them once and for all but also help you begin on a path you may not have ever found the entrance to before, the path to financial freedom!

12 Keys to Getting Out of Debt

1. Consider the benefits of being debt free!

Picture a life without debt. You wake up in the morning and can't believe how well you slept last night. The reason you slept so well is because you have eliminated debt from your life. You know that today there will be no calls or mail demanding payment. You won't have to look at the pile of bills in front of you and try to decide, "OK, which bills are bugging me the most" or "which bills am I going to pay this month." As a matter of fact, you paid bills just last night. You paid each one, without any concern whether there is enough money or where will the money come from to pay this bill?

Imagine having breakfast with your wife and you say, "What would you like to do today?" She, of course, says she'd like to go shopping and buy wallpaper for the kitchen. With a smile, you say OK, let's go. You know you already have the money set aside for this project. No longer

Notes:

_____

_____

_____

_____

do you have to examine your charge cards for the one with enough credit to allow another purchase. The money is already there!

You have also noticed that you two no longer seem to fight as much. Your marriage has never been better! That night, your daughter, who is a senior in high school, begins to talk about what college she would like to attend. Again, you smile because you have no debt and you also built enough of a net-worth while getting out of debt that provides for her college education.

Instead of saying to your daughter she has to be really smart and get a scholarship, you can begin to talk to her about her life and career goals. When the car breaks down, you have money set aside for just such an unexpected expense!

For the first time in your life this Christmas or holiday you enjoyed the feeling of paying cash rather than using debt and spending the entire next year (or longer) to pay it off! Being debt free is worth the effort!

2.   Set a goal and create a freedom plan to be financially free.

This book is not on the subject of goals. However, nothing can motivate you more than having goals in life. A goal can be exhilarating! A goal puts a timetable on when you can expect to be financially free. It's like seeing the light at the end of the tunnel. You work hard to reach the light. The closer you get to the light, the harder you work and more motivated you become because you can see the light! It gets brighter and more exciting the closer you get. Find out how long it will take you to get debt free, prepare a freedom plan. Then prepare to get excited! It won't take nearly as long as you think.

Notes:

_____

_____

_____

_____

3. Plan to invest a percentage of each paycheck!

This will be the subject in a later chapter. However, building your net worth is something that comes from making investing an automatic part of your financial life.

4. List everything you owe.

You need to list every debt that you currently have. I mean everything! List them starting at the top with the debt that has the smallest balance leading down to the last one which is your greatest debt. Many advisors teach listing the debt with the highest interest rate first and making that debt your highest priority. In a small number of cases, this could be accurate. For most cases, I disagree! Always list the smallest debt first, regardless of interest rate. Later in this chapter, I will be going into detail on this issue and why this is so important.

5. List everything you own.

Again, I mean list everything! The old computer you have stored in the basement you no longer use. The old set of golf clubs. The wheelbarrow. The record player or turntable you replaced with a CD player. The old TV, the craft items you no longer decorate with, your jewelry. You need to list everything you can think of. Once your list is complete, then...

Notes:

_____

_____

_____

_____

6. Have a sale!

Today there are more ways than ever to have a sale. No longer are you restricted to your neighborhood garage sale and what local folks are willing to pay. A garage sale is still a viable means to sell many of your goods that you no longer use. However, don't overlook the Internet. There are auctions available everywhere you turn. For your nicer items, give the web a try. If you are not computer savvy, then find a friend who is. Keep in mind your local church or place of worship! They can provide someone who will help or direct you to someone who can.

Obviously the money raised from the sales can help you on the road to being debt and financially free. It takes the light at the end of the tunnel and brings it a lot closer in the blink of an eye. Can you feel it? Here comes that exciting feeling!

7. Live on a cash basis.

Later in this chapter, I will be telling you how to plan ahead so that you can pay for all your needs with cash instead of credit. It's a few simple steps that anyone can implement. It makes a huge difference in your mindset as well.

8. Create added income projects to inhance your freedom plan.

Everyone has some skill or ability that can be turned into cash! Even if you added just another $100 per month of income that went toward your debt and financial portfolio, you will soon enjoy the impact this can have on your financial future. Network marketing companies can be a great source of added income.

Notes:

_____

_____

_____

_____

43

They can provide proven ways to generate income with little or no start up cost, and most of the materials needed for your business are already produced and available to you.

9. Dedicate a monthly amount to pay off debt.

Remember, you will be investing at the same time you are paying off your debt. The extra money we put toward debt will go to our obligation with the lowest balance regardless of the interest rate. Then as each creditor is paid off, take the monthly payment paid to them and add it to the next debt on the list. Again, I will give you detailed examples of how to do this later in this chapter.

10. Write each creditor with your repayment plan and schedule and keep a copy.

In addition to becoming debt-free and building your financial portfolio, you must make sure to protect or restore your credit rating. This can become very important later when you begin to find alternative sources of income. Later, when you are debt free, you may need the help of a banker in beginning a business of your own or maybe buying some real estate. Therefore, make sure you communicate with your creditors. I have found that most every creditor is more understanding and much easier to work with when you communicate.

11. Stick to your freedom plan.

Imagine an engineer who is building a skyscraper who decides to change some of the measurements in the architectural plans. The building would

Notes:

_____

_____

_____

_____

be unsafe, dangerous and may never support itself. The same is true of your plan. While from time to time adjustments may be needed (you suddenly generate added income or have a loss of income), never give up on the plan. Make the adjustments and move on. Don't give up! In the words of Winston Churchill: "Never, never, never give up!"

12. Find a mentor.

Whenever you embark on a plan such as this, there will be times when you have to make some decisions pertaining to certain areas of your freedom plan. It is important to have someone you trust to turn to for an outside opinion.

Sometimes you will be tempted to alter your plan in an inappropriate way. Your old habits may want to creep back in and take over. You need someone who can recognize this and slap some common sense back into you!

I have been working with some options trading this year more than ever before. Options can be a risky investment in the market. I don't recommend them for any beginner to investing. During any form of investing, it can be very easy to let your emotions take control instead of following your plan. You must decide when investing in areas of risk, what your entrance point is (at what price you will buy) and what your exit point is (at what price you will sell). Otherwise you can become emotionally attached to the investment and it becomes harder to make the right decisions.

I decided at the onset of the options trading to get a partner. Bruce, one of my dearest friends and I met every other Tuesday to compare ideas

Notes:

_____

_____

_____

_____

and make sure we were staying on track with our investment plan. I remember one time when Bruce had doubled his money on an option over two days. We spoke by phone that day and I asked him if he wanted to sell: He started to waver and think about how much more money he could make if he just held on a bit longer. I asked him if he hit his exit point, if doubling his money achieved the goal he had set when he bought it? He said yes, but… And I said "Oink, Oink!" He made the decision to sell. That same day after he sold, the stock began a downward spiral and has not stopped as of this writing. Don't get me wrong. There have been plenty of times when I was the one wavering with emotion and Bruce came to my rescue.

Maybe you could recommend this book to a friend who may be in the same position as yourself. They could be a great partner for you as you learn. You could also approach a parent or family member whom you respect and trust. I would have them to read this book in order to understand your freedom plan and why you are doing things the way you are.

How To Begin Your Financial Freedom Plan!

Step #1:   Identify Current Cash Flow

The first step is to figure out where your money is currently going. How, where, why and what are you spending it on? On the next few pages, you will find an "Identify Your Current Cash Flow" guide.

You need to begin by gathering all of your current bills. A good way to make sure you're not missing any is to review your checkbook and credit card statements.

Notes:

_____

_____

_____

_____

The first key is to break everything down into monthly amounts. For example, if you pay your life insurance quarterly, divide it by three to come up with a monthly amount. **Everything must be broken down monthly!** If you get paid every two weeks, you would multiply that by 26 times per year and then divide by 12.

Example

Salary	$2,000.00 every two weeks	=	$4,333.33 mo.
Bonus	$1,000.00 every other month	=	$ 500.00 mo.
Life Ins.	$ 300.00 every six months	=	$ 50.00 mo.

At the very end of the exercise, you will subtract your expenses from your income. Hopefully, there's something left over. If not, then you need to have a sale or create more cash flow (mentioned earlier) to reduce debt and increase income. It's possible a part-time job may be necessary. However, I have found that in most cases an additional job is not needed when the Freedom Plan is followed. Later in Step #2, I will be providing more ideas for you to save or earn more.

Notes:

_____

_____

_____

_____

STEP #1:

IDENTIFY YOUR CURRENT CASH FLOW

DO NOT list your net income...Write in your gross income before taxes. We will be listing taxes withheld in another location.

EXAMPLE:

Salary / Wages #1	$ 1,850.00 *per*	2 weeks	= $ 3,700.00 *per month*
Salary/ Wages #2	$ 2,083.33 *per*	Month	= $ 2,083.33 *per month*
Bonuses/ Commissions	$ 500.00 *per*	Month	= $ 500.00 *per month*
Other Income	$ 1,500.00 *per*	6 Months	= $ 250.00 *per month*
TOTAL EARNED INCOME:			$ 6,533.33 *per month*

Then...list all your expenses in the spaces provided, recalculating non-monthly expenses to fit a monthly time frame.

EXAMPLE:

Auto Insurance $ 800.00   *per*   *6 Months* = $ 133.00   *per month*

When you have totaled all your income and expenses, subtract your average monthly expenses from your monthly income. This number is your discretionary income.

EXAMPLE:

Total Monthly Income	$ 6,533.33
Total Monthly Expenses	- $ 5,333.33
Current Monthly Discretionary Income	$ 1,200.00

Worksheet - Page 1

EARNED INCOME

Salary / Wages #1 $ _____ per _____ = $ _____ per month

Salary / Wages #2 $ _____ per _____ = $ _____ per month

Bonuses/
Commissions $ _____ per _____ = $ _____ per month

TOTAL EARNED INCOME $ _____ per month

UNEARNED INCOME

Interest Income $ _____ per _____ = $ _____ per month

Dividends $ _____ per _____ = $ _____ per month

Alimony $ _____ per _____ = $ _____ per month

Child Support $ _____ per _____ = $ _____ per month

Other $ _____ per _____ = $ _____ per month

TOTAL UNEARNED INCOME $ _____ per month

TOTAL MONTHLY INCOME $ _____ per month

Worksheet - Page 2

EXPENSES

FICA/
Self Employment $ _____ per _____ = $ _____ per month

Federal Withholding $ _____ per _____ = $ _____ per month

State Withholding $ _____ per _____ = $ _____ per month

Property $ _____ per _____ = $ _____ per month

Other $ _____ per _____ = $ _____ per month

TOTAL MONTHLY TAXES $ _____ per month

**MEDICAL /
DENTAL**

Doctor $ _____ per _____ = $ _____ per month

Dentist $ _____ per _____ = $ _____ per month

Hospital / Lab $ _____ per _____ = $ _____ per month

Drugs / Medicine $ _____ per _____ = $ _____ per month

Other $ _____ per _____ = $ _____ per month

TOTAL MONTHLY MEDICAL/DENTAL $ _____ per month

**CONTRIBUTIONS /
DONATIONS**

Church $ _____ per _____ = $ _____ per month

Charitable Org.'s $ _____ per _____ = $ _____ per month

Other $ _____ per _____ = $ _____ per month

TOTAL MONTHLY DONATIONS $ _____ per month

Worksheet - Page 3

EXPENSES

Payments

Home Mortgage	$ _____ per _____	= $ _____	per month
Mortgage #2	$ _____ per _____	= $ _____	per month
Home Rental	$ _____ per _____	= $ _____	per month
Car Loan #1	$ _____ per _____	= $ _____	per month
Car Loan #2	$ _____ per _____	= $ _____	per month
Car Loan #3	$ _____ per _____	= $ _____	per month
Car Loan #4	$ _____ per _____	= $ _____	per month
Other	$ _____ per _____	= $ _____	per month

TOTAL MONTHLY PAYMENTS $ _____ per month

Insurance

Life Insurance	$ _____ per _____	= $ _____	per month
Auto Insurance	$ _____ per _____	= $ _____	per month
Home Insurance	$ _____ per _____	= $ _____	per month
Medical Insurance	$ _____ per _____	= $ _____	per month
Dental Insurance	$ _____ per _____	= $ _____	per month
Other Insurance	$ _____ per _____	= $ _____	per month

TOTAL MONTHLY INSURANCE $ _____ per month

Worksheet - Page 4

EXPENSES

Household

Dry Cleaning/ Laundry	$ _____ per _____	= $ _____ per month
Electricity	$ _____ per _____	= $ _____ per month
Natural Gas	$ _____ per _____	= $ _____ per month
Water	$ _____ per _____	= $ _____ per month
Cell Phone	$ _____ per _____	= $ _____ per month
Telephone	$ _____ per _____	= $ _____ per month
Groceries	$ _____ per _____	= $ _____ per month
Other	$ _____ per _____	= $ _____ per month

TOTAL MONTHLY HOUSEHOLD $ _____ per month

Personal

Accounting/ Tax Preparation	$ _____ per _____	= $ _____ per month
Alimony	$ _____ per _____	= $ _____ per month
Babysitting	$ _____ per _____	= $ _____ per month
Bank Service Chgs	$ _____ per _____	= $ _____ per month
Child Care	$ _____ per _____	= $ _____ per month
Child Support	$ _____ per _____	= $ _____ per month
Children's Allowance	$ _____ per _____	= $ _____ per month
Children's School Expenses	$ _____ per _____	= $ _____ per month
Clothing	$ _____ per _____	= $ _____ per month
Dine Out	$ _____ per _____	= $ _____ per month
Dues/ Subscriptions	$ _____ per _____	= $ _____ per month
Education/ Tuition	$ _____ per _____	= $ _____ per month
Entertainment	$ _____ per _____	= $ _____ per month

Worksheet - Page 5

Personal (cont'd)

Gifts $ _____ per _____ = $ _____ per month

Hair/ Personal Care $ _____ per _____ = $ _____ per month

Hobbies $ _____ per _____ = $ _____ per month

Home Furnishings $ _____ per _____ = $ _____ per month

Home Improvements $ _____ per _____ = $ _____ per month

Home Maintenance $ _____ per _____ = $ _____ per month

I.R.A. $ _____ per _____ = $ _____ per month

Legal Costs $ _____ per _____ = $ _____ per month

Pension Contribution $ _____ per _____ = $ _____ per month

Pet Care $ _____ per _____ = $ _____ per month

Postage/Stationery $ _____ per _____ = $ _____ per month

Recreation/ Sports $ _____ per _____ = $ _____ per month

Vacation $ _____ per _____ = $ _____ per month

Vehicle Gas/ Oil $ _____ per _____ = $ _____ per month

Vehicle Licensing $ _____ per _____ = $ _____ per month

Vehicle Maintenance $ _____ per _____ = $ _____ per month

Vehicle Wash/ Wax $ _____ per _____ = $ _____ per month

Other $ _____ per _____ = $ _____ per month

Other $ _____ per _____ = $ _____ per month

Other $ _____ per _____ = $ _____ per month

Other $ _____ per _____ = $ _____ per month

Other $ _____ per _____ = $ _____ per month

Other $ _____ per _____ = $ _____ per month

Other $ _____ per _____ = $ _____ per month

TOTAL MONTHLY PERSONAL $ _____ per month

TOTAL MONTHLY EXPENSES $ _____

TOTAL MONTHLY INCOME (from worksheet page 1) $ _____

TOTAL MONTHLY EXPENSES (from worksheet page 4) $ _____

CURRENT MONTHLY DISCRETIONARY INCOME $ _____

Step #2:   Create and find additional cash flow

Identify different ways to increase your monthly cash flow by reducing how much you spend and increasing how much new income you generate.

A.   Identify ways to reduce your expenses.

Stop paying for cable for just a while. Many people have a monthly cable bill of $50 to $75 per month. At the very least, you could go to basic cable and save $20-$40/month.
Est. Savings: $40/month

Cancel the newspaper.
Est. Savings: $20/month.

Change Automobiles.   Your current payment might be $400 to $500/month. Why not sell your car and buy another with a reduced payment of $300 to $400/month.
Est. Savings: $100/month

Change your phone service. With so many phone companies and the dropping rates, you could possibly find service for half of the price you are now paying. All it takes is a little investigation.
Est. Savings: $20/month

Find a part time job or business. Many companies are looking for part-time help as they realize the savings to the company. Companies save by not having to provide benefits. Also, part-time help can mean lower taxes and lower insurance costs to the company.

Notes:

_____

_____

_____

_____

An option to working outside the home part-time is to begin your own business within your home. I have met one person making custom drapery. Others I have met are doing things like:

- Repairing cars
- Installing drywall
- Repairing computers
- Cleaning homes
- Building, or creating products to sell at street fairs.

The ideas are unlimited. To find more ideas, you may want to check on your computer or at the library. On the computer, simply type "working from home" in your search engine on the internet. At the library, simply ask the librarian to direct you to the many books written on working from home.

There are many network marketing companies providing business ideas that can be done from your home. It's similar to buying your own franchise. You don't have to create anything. They have done all the work for you. They provide the product line and the business plan. They also will provide the mentors and guidance to help you build your business. Make sure they have quality products for you to sell or market. If not, it could be illegal.

In whatever you decide to do, make sure you check with the Better Business Bureau in your area for any possible complaints. Also, you can call the Attorney General's office in your state to further investigate. While any of the ideas you find could provide substantial incomes, let's be conservative. Assume you made an extra $30 per week.

Notes:

_____

_____

_____

Est. Earnings: $120/mo.

In appendix "B," you'll find a chart that may be helpful in developing and identifying extra cash flow.

<u>Step #3:</u>   The Sale

As just stated in point #6 above, sell whatever you can. The idea is to raise as much money as possible to pay toward your smallest balance of debt. Always begin by paying off the debt with the lowest balance first. This goes against most teachings on debt reduction. You may have heard before, that you always put your money first toward the card with the highest interest rate. That is not always the best move!

In most every case I have seen, the highest balance of a client's credit cards is usually the one with the highest interest rate. There's a reason they allow you to carry such a high balance; they are charging you the top interest rates! If you chose to pay off the highest balance first, the one with the highest interest rate, how long will it be before you have any sense of success by getting rid of a credit card? It may take you two years before you cut up your first credit card! That's a long, long, long time!

Think of it this way, let's say you were going on a diet to lose weight. You entered your weight loss program and the person counseling you says, "Now you won't lose even one pound for about two years. However, don't lose hope! Stick with the plan because once you lose the first pound, the rest will fall off quickly." Question. How long would you last on that diet? I want results!

Notes:

_____

_____

_____

_____

By contrast, you go to the competition. They have a different plan for losing weight. On this plan, they inform you that it costs a bit more than the first plan. However, you will lose weight almost immediately. After one day, you will be down two pounds. By the end of the first week, you will have lost six pounds. By the end of the first month, you will have lost 20 pounds. This diet may cost a tad more, but what are your chances of success?

When it comes to getting out of debt and building your net worth, you need some successes along the way to motivate you to continue with your plan. Therefore, you pay off the smallest balance first. Then the next smallest and so on without regard to the interest rate you're paying on each.

You may say, "But Curt, won't I being paying a whole bunch more in interest?" It will take 34 months to be debt free by paying off the lowest balance first. Paying off the highest balance card first would take 32 months and you would save $622.40 of interest over the three and a half years of payments. However, I believe the extra $622.40 of interest and two extra months are worth the early success of seeing those cards be destroyed.

Remember the weight loss plan that cost a bit more, but worked! It's called motivation and it can be the key to your success. If you never see your first success for 25 months, then it becomes easier to give up on your goal. Therefore, make sure you lay out your debts beginning with the lowest balance to be paid off first and working up to the highest balance being paid off last.

Notes:

_____

_____

_____

_____

Anyway, who says you have to pay that extra $622.40 of interest? How many times do you recall receiving a new credit card offer in the mail? I mean the ones that say "zero interest for one full year on transfers." They show up in your mailbox almost every month if not every week. Even if your credit isn't the best, with so many offers, there's a good chance you would be accepted. You can knock off a tremendous amount of interest by taking advantage of the one year at zero interest. You may say, well yeah, but in one year what's the rate? Before one year is up, do it again with another card for a second year of no interest. Trust me, another opportunity will always be in your mailbox. Just make sure each time you get a new card, dispose the old card and call or write to close the account. Some debt advisors recommend you collect or build up a file of credit cards. I feel like this is telling an alcoholic to collect fine scotch and whiskey, but don't ever drink them. By finding cards with zero interest for each year, now the 42 vs. 44- month payoff plan is meaningless. You never paid interest! If you paid no interest, then why would you go with option one?

It is critical in a debt reduction plan to have some successes as quickly as possible to encourage you to continue with your plan! Nothing feels better than cutting up your first credit card. Nothing is better than a steady habit of doing that along the way. Try waiting two years to cut up your first card and see how you feel. Again, the end result in how many dollars it takes to get debt free by paying off the smallest balance first is nominal. So, always pay off the lowest balance first! I'll show you more on this in a moment. For now, however, let's look at the "Freedom Plan"!

Notes:

_____

_____

_____

_____

Step #4   The Freedom Plan

Let's say your lowest balance is Tire City. Winter was coming and you knew you needed new tires in the bad weather. Rather than gamble with your safety, you bought the tires on the Tire City credit card. Your balance is $655.

Now let's assume you found a bunch of stuff in the attic, garage or basement to sell on Ebay or some other online auction or garage sale. It's very possible you could raise the entire $655 to pay off your first credit card. This would free up the $25 monthly payment you were making. Now, the key is each time you pay off one card, you take the payment from that card and add it to the payment you have been making on the second card. This way you pay off the second card that much faster. If the payment on your second card is $35 per month, by adding the $25 freed up from the first card that's now paid off, you are making payments to the tune of $60 per month on the second card. OOOOOHHH it feels good! Once you have paid off credit card #2, you then take the payment from both card #1 and #2 ($60) and add that to your payment on debt #3. On debt #3, you were paying $40 per month. By adding the extra $60 per month now available from the first two cards to the $40 on debt #3, your paying $100 per month to debt #3. You then continue this process until all of your debt is gone!

OK, you did it! You had a sale. You came up with $655 to put toward debt. You also worked hard and between changing some of your payments and finding a way to earn a few extra dollars a week, you came up with an extra $300 per month to put toward your financial freedom plan!

Notes:

_____

_____

_____

_____

The Key

Many financial advisors would tell you to take the extra $300 and put it all toward debt. While this strategy can accomplish helping you get out of debt, it does little to correct the problem permanently. My experience has shown it seldom works! How motivating is it to spend the next two, three maybe even five years of your life taking every penny you can muster up and do nothing but pay off debt?

Most people begin with a high level of determination. You say, "I'm getting out of debt this time!" However, the more time goes on, the more you lose hope and get tired of always being broke and never having any money or fun. You need something exciting to happen at the same time your paying off debt. You need something to continue to motivate you to stay the course.

Imagine what would it feel like, if while you were paying down a debt, one day you received a statement of your investment portfolio that said you had almost $2,000 in investments at the end of your first year of paying off debt? You've tried before, but have never been able to save. Suddenly, in the midst of becoming debt free, you're doing it! That doesn't make sense, you say. How can I be doing something I have never been able to do before, save money **while paying off my debt?**
Six months later, your investment is now worth about $3,000! By the time you pay off all your debts, say in three and a half years, you now have between $7,500 and $10,000 in your investment portfolio. All while becoming debt free!

Suddenly, you don't get so depressed. As a matter of fact, the faster your investments grow in value, the more excited you get. You've never been

Notes:

_____

_____

_____

_____

able to save money before. So, as your investments grow, you get excited about finding ways to feed the growth! Your focus has now shifted to where you never, ever again want the feeling of being in debt. The feeling of seeing your net worth and investment portfolio grow is more exciting, and you get this desire to never let debt creep back into your life again!

Without a positive move in your investments, what's going to keep you from going into debt again? I mean, fine! Let's say you're one of the rare ones who does pay off all your debt. Have your habits that first got you into debt changed? Most likely they have not. The reason is you never did anything to change your way of handling money. Under the traditional system of paying off debt, by the time you are out of debt (should you be one of the few who actually accomplishes it) you are so sick and tired of being in debt and doing nothing but paying toward it, that you decide to celebrate and take the family to Disney World on a much needed vacation. How do you pay for it? YOU CHARGE IT! Why not? You have no other way to pay and your cards all have a zero balance now. You see, the habits haven't changed! Over time you manage to find yourself back in debt again. Looking back to your last struggle with debt, you realize how hard it was for three to five years.

You remember the pain of being in debt. Now, you can't muster up the determination to start all over again.

The "Freedom Plan" will teach you to become debt free. And, at the same time, you will be building your investment portfolio and be increasing your net worth. Most importantly, you will be changing your habits! Once your investments climb to levels you never thought you could achieve, your focus will shift from accumulating more debt to

Notes:

_____

_____

_____

_____

finding more money to invest. You will become more determined than ever to not go into debt again.

I propose that if you take a person "who just can't seem to save," and help them do what they felt they couldn't, that is build a substantial financial net worth, not only will they become avid savers and investors, but they will also stay out of debt for the rest of their lives.

Debt Free Or Financially Free?

Below is a typical persons debt list:

Account Name	Current Balance	Monthly Payment	Annual Interest	Months To Pay	Total Interest
1. Tire City	$ 655	$ 30	21.000	27.7	$ 177.46
2. Home Depot	$ 867	$ 35	18.000	31.2	$ 225.02
3. Parisian	$1,807	$ 50	19.000	54.1	$ 895.66
4. Community Visa	$3,333	$ 50	16.000	165.8	$ 4958.48
5. First USA	$4,335	$100	13.500	59.8	$ 1,643.43
6. Bank of America	$5,001	$100	21.000	119.9	$ 6,993.29
TOTALS	$15,998	$365			$14,893.35

Notes:

_____

_____

_____

_____

The Split

You need to split the monthly amount you have come up with for your "Freedom Plan." Based on our illustration, you have found an extra $300 per month to put toward your plan. $150 of the monthly amount needs to go toward paying off your debt as shown earlier. The other $150 per month will be invested. You may be thinking, how can saving a measly $150 per month help me be financially free? Don't I need at least $10,000 or more to begin investing? The Bible says, "He who gathers money little by little, makes it grow" (Proverbs 13:11).

As I counsel people over the age of 50, I find in many cases the most sizable portion of their retirement assets have come from their savings plan through their employer. Why? Because money was automatically taken out of their paycheck and they never saw it. They learned to live on the leftover amount. It's those small monthly contributions that make all the difference! Building your assets, financial net worth and future is every bit as important as paying off your debt. The problem with only paying off your debt is it doesn't teach you how to save, invest and build your net worth.

You'll Never Have Financial Freedom By Paying Off Your Debt!

Most people have a self-imposed figure in their head of how much debt they are comfortable with. For some of us it is zero debt, for some $2,000; for others its $10,000 or more. Let's say your comfort zone is at $2,000. You've run across some hard times recently and were "forced" to increase your debt to pay for "necessary" items. You now find your

Notes:

_____

_____

_____

_____

debts totaling $10,000. This is not in your comfort zone. Therefore, you pull in your belt and begin to focus on getting the debt back down. After several months of hard work and some overtime, you manage to get your debt down to or near the $2,000 level. Now you begin to feel better, less stressed and comfortable with spending money once again. The cycle starts all over. Debt is a cycle that continues to repeat itself. The point is, as long as you wait until you are debt free to begin investing (as most advisors would tell you to do), you most likely never will.

I can't tell you the number of times I have heard people say; "As soon as I get these last few debts paid off, then I'm planning on starting to invest." Baloney! As soon as they get their debts back down to their comfort zone, they now feel free to start spending again. It's the only way they ever see themselves having anything in life.

Remember one of the greatest motivators in becoming debt free is to see early success! You have two options in paying down this debt.

Option One (No Split)

Assume you take the extra $300 per month you've found and put it all toward debt. Also assume, that you pay off the debt with the highest balance first. You would be debt free in 32 months. You won't be able to cut up your first card for 25 months (over 2 years). How motivating is that? Your second card would be cut up after 36 months (3 years!).

Notes:

_____

_____

_____

_____

Option Two

Now, let's say you split the extra $300 per month. You put $150 of it toward the lowest balance debt you have first.

This is how your payoff would look:

Month #/ Acct. Name	Balance	Annual Interest	Payment
MONTH #1			
1. Tire City	$ 655.00	$ 11.46	$180.00
2. Home Depot	$ 867.00	$ 13.01	$ 35.00
3. Parisian	$ 1,807.00	$ 28.61	$ 50.00
4. Community Visa	$ 3,333.00	$ 44.44	$ 50.00
5. First USA	$ 4,335.00	$ 48.77	$100.00
6. Bank of America	$ 5,001.00	$ 87.52	$100.00
MONTH TOTALS	*$15,998.00*	*$233.80*	*$515.00*
MONTH #2			
1. Tire City	$ 486.46	$ 8.51	$180.00
2. Home Depot	$ 845.01	$ 12.68	$ 35.00
3. Parisian	$ 1,785.61	$ 28.27	$ 50.00
4. Community Visa	$ 3,327.44	$ 44.37	$ 50.00
5. First USA	$ 4,283.77	$ 48.19	$100.00
6. Bank of America	$ 4,988.52	$ 87.30	$100.00
MONTH TOTALS	*$15,716.80*	*$229.32*	*$515.00*

$30
+ $150
▼ *extra payment*

Notes:

_____

_____

_____

_____

Month #/ Acct. Name	Balance	Annual Interest	Payment
MONTH #3			
1. Tire City	$ 314.98	$ 5.51	$180.00
2. Home Depot	$ 822.68	$ 12.34	$ 35.00
3. Parisian	$ 1,763.88	$ 27.93	$ 50.00
4. Community Visa	$ 3,321.81	$ 44.29	$ 50.00
5. First USA	$ 4,231.96	$ 47.61	$100.00
6. Bank of America	$ 4,975.82	$ 87.08	$100.00
MONTH TOTALS	*$15,431.12*	*$224.76*	*$515.00*
MONTH #4			
1. Tire City	$ 140.49	$ 2.46	$142.95
2. Home Depot	$ 800.02	$ 12.00	$ 72.05
3. Parisian	$ 1,741.81	$ 27.58	$ 50.00
4. Community Visa	$ 3,316.10	$ 44.21	$ 50.00
5. First USA	$ 4,179.57	$ 47.02	$100.00
6. Bank of America	$ 4,962.89	$ 86.85	$100.00
MONTH TOTALS	*$15,140.88*	*$220.12*	*$515.00*
MONTH #5			
1. Home Depot	$ 739.97	$ 11.10	$215.00
2. Parisian	$ 1,719.39	$ 27.22	$ 50.00
3. Community Visa	$ 3,310.11	$ 44.14	$ 50.00
4. First USA	$ 4,126.59	$ 46.42	$100.00
5. Bank of America	$ 4,949.74	$ 86.62	$100.00
MONTH TOTALS	*$14,846.51*	*$215.51*	*$515.00*

Payoff Amount

$30
+$35
+ $150
extra pymt.

Notes:

_____

_____

_____

_____

Month #/ Acct. Name	Balance	Annual Interest	Payment
MONTH #6			
1. Home Depot	$ 536.07	$ 8.04	$215.00
2. Parisian	$ 1,696.61	$ 26.86	$ 50.00
3. Community Visa	$ 3,304.45	$ 44.06	$ 50.00
4. First USA	$ 4,073.01	$ 45.82	$100.00
5. Bank of America	$ 4,936.36	$ 86.39	$100.00
MONTH TOTALS	*$14,546.51*	*$211.17*	*$515.00*
MONTH #7			
1. Home Depot	$ 329.11	$ 4.94	$215.00
2. Parisian	$ 1,673.48	$ 26.50	$ 50.00
3. Community Visa	$ 3,298.51	$ 43.98	$ 50.00
4. First USA	$ 4,018.84	$ 45.21	$100.00
5. Bank of America	$ 4,922.75	$ 86.15	$100.00
MONTH TOTALS	*$14,242.68*	*$206.77*	*$515.00*
MONTH #8			
1. Home Depot	$ 119.05	$ 1.79	$120.84
2. Parisian	$ 1,649.97	$ 26.12	$144.16
3. Community Visa	$ 3,292.49	$ 43.90	$ 50.00
4. First USA	$ 3,964.05	$ 44.60	$100.00
5. Bank of America	$ 4,908.90	$ 85.91	$100.00
MONTH TOTALS	*$13,934.45*	*$202.31*	*$515.00*

Payoff Amount

Notes:

_____

_____

_____

_____

Month #/ Acct. Name	Balance	Annual Interest	Payment
MONTH #9			
1. Parisian	$ 1,531.93	$ 24.26	$265.00
2. Community Visa	$ 3,286.39	$ 43.82	$ 50.00
3. First USA	$ 3,908.64	$ 43.97	$100.00
4. Bank of America	$ 4,894.80	$ 85.66	$100.00
MONTH TOTALS	*$13,621.77*	*$197.71*	*$515.00*
MONTH #10			
1. Parisian	$ 1,291.19	$ 20.44	$265.00
2. Community Visa	$ 3,280.21	$ 43.74	$ 50.00
3. First USA	$ 3,852.62	$ 43.34	$100.00
4. Bank of America	$ 4,880.46	$ 85.41	$100.00
MONTH TOTALS	*$13,304.47*	*$192.93*	*$515.00*
MONTH #11			
1. Parisian	$ 1,046.63	$ 16.57	$265.00
2. Community Visa	$ 3,273.94	$ 43.65	$ 50.00
3. First USA	$ 3,795.96	$ 42.70	$100.00
4. Bank of America	$ 4,865.87	$ 85.15	$100.00
MONTH TOTALS	*$12,982.40*	*$188.08*	*$515.00*
MONTH #12			
1. Parisian	$ 798.20	$ 12.64	$265.00
2. Community Visa	$ 3,267.60	$ 43.57	$ 50.00
3. First USA	$ 3,738.66	$ 42.06	$100.00
4. Bank of America	$ 4,851.02	$ 84.89	$100.00
MONTH TOTALS	*$12,655.49*	*$183.16*	*$515.00*

$30
+ $35
+ $50
+ $150 extra
payment

Notes:

_____

_____

_____

_____

Let's assume, instead of putting the entire $300 per month extra toward debt, that we split it. We put $150 toward debt reduction and invested the other $150.

If you put the entire $300 per month toward debt, you would be out of debt in 32 months and have paid $4,739 in interest. If you paid $150 per month toward your debt reduction, it would take you 44 months to be debt-free and you would have paid $6,517 in interest. That means you would have paid an extra $1,778 in extra interest.

However, assume you invested the other $150 per month into a stock mutual fund averaging a rate of return of 10% per year. At the end of 44 months you would have a balance of $7,719 in your investment portfolio. Would you trade $1,778 in interest for $7,719 in an investment portfolio? My guess is yes! If you continued to invest just the $150 per month extra, after becoming debt free, in 10 more years your investment would be worth $51,622. In 20 years over $170,470, and in 30 years over $492,198.

There are three reasons why this plan is OK. First, I believe the extra $1,778 of interest and extra months are worth the early success of seeing those cards be destroyed.

Remember the weight loss plan that cost a bit more, but worked! It's called motivation and it can be the key to your success. If you never see your first success for 25 months, then it becomes easier to give up on your goal. Therefore, make sure you lay out your debts beginning with the lowest balance to be paid off first and working up to the highest balance being paid off last. Do you want a plan that works? Or, do you want one that saves a few bucks and has a high percentage of failure?

Notes:

_____

_____

_____

_____

Secondly, who says you have to pay the extra interest anyway? Earlier in this chapter, I showed a way to use zero interest rate credit cards while paying off your debt. By finding cards with zero interest for each year, now the 44-month payoff plan is meaningless. You never paid interest! If you paid no interest, then why would you go with option one?

The third reason it's OK is the extra $7,719 in my pocket! I need to say the same would be true if you paid off your debt in 32 months and then invested the $655 extra for the last 12 months. However, would you do it? My experience has taught me that in every case (with rare…and I mean rare occasion) the answer is no! As soon as most people get close to debt free, they begin to charge again! We all need motivation to save and then not touch what we've saved. The plan we have just laid out <u>will</u> help you succeed!

I believe (and have seen it happen time and time again) when someone who has never been able to save before, finally gets a nest egg of $8,000 to $10,000 or more, it becomes the golden egg. You are so proud to have been able to save money for your future, that you are now scared to death of blowing that money. Not only that, but the bigger your nest egg gets, the more excited you become about putting more into it, and the less interest you have in more debt. It's fun to watch your money grow!

Notes:

_____

_____

_____

_____

Let's take it one step further. Assume at the point you pay off your debt, you take the total debt payment of $682 per month (you've been paying it for 44 months anyway) and you decide to invest it in your stock mutual fund. Remember, you already have a balance of $7,719 to begin with.

Here's what happens:

Year	Beginning Bal.	Ending Bal.
1	$7,719	$ 17,097
5		$ 65,512
10		$ 160,599
20		$ 574,455
30		$1,694,778

Now that's a nest egg! Paying off your debt while building your financial net worth is the key to financial freedom!

The Cost of Waiting

To best illustrate the value of time, let's look at two good friends of mine. Allow me to introduce you to Procrastinator Pete and Eagar Eddie. Eddie got his first good job at age 21. He was in the bookstore one day and found a book on the subject of investing. After reading it, he was convinced it would be a good idea to begin investing some money right away. Even though the job was a good one, Eddie still found that the best he could do would be to save about $1,000 per year or about $83 per month. Around the age of 28, Eddie found the girl of his dreams and got married. They decided to purchase a house and start a family right away. This made it extremely hard for Eddie to keep saving his $83 per month. So, he postponed any further investing until things

Notes:

_____

_____

_____

_____

improved. However, Eddie never again was able to invest anything. He only invested a total of $8,000.

Procrastinator Pete on the other hand was in the same boat as Eddie, in the beginning. Pete was 21 and had landed a great job as well. However, Pete had one thing on his mind. He was ready to live baby! He went right out and bought a brand new car and began to travel and see the world. When Pete was 28, he had seen many exotic places and through the help of a friend, began to see the need to begin investing. So, like Eddie, he began to invest the same $83 per month/$1,000 per year. Pete was very diligent however and continued to invest each month from age 28 all the way through to age 65, saving a total of $37,000 compared to Eddie's $8,000.

Question? Who was smarter? Who came out ahead? Eddie did!

Notes:

_____

_____

_____

_____

The Cost Of Waiting
Values at 10%

Age	Eddie		Value/Year		Pete		Value/Year
21	$1,000.00	$	1,100.00			$	-
22	$1,000.00	$	2,310.00			$	-
23	$1,000.00	$	3,641.00			$	-
24	$1,000.00	$	5,105.10			$	-
25	$1,000.00	$	6,715.61			$	-
26	$1,000.00	$	8,487.17			$	-
27	$1,000.00	$	10,435.89			$	-
28	$1,000.00	$	12,579.48			$	-
29		$	13,837.42	$	1,000.00	$	1,100.00
30		$	15,221.17	$	1,000.00	$	2,310.00
31		$	16,743.28	$	1,000.00	$	3,641.00
32		$	18,417.61	$	1,000.00	$	5,105.10
33		$	20,259.37	$	1,000.00	$	6,715.61
34		$	22,285.31	$	1,000.00	$	8,487.17
35		$	24,513.84	$	1,000.00	$	10,435.89
36		$	26,965.23	$	1,000.00	$	12,579.48
37		$	29,661.75	$	1,000.00	$	14,937.42
38		$	32,627.92	$	1,000.00	$	17,531.17
39		$	35,890.72	$	1,000.00	$	20,384.28
40		$	39,479.79	$	1,000.00	$	23,522.71
41		$	43,427.77	$	1,000.00	$	26,974.98
42		$	47,770.54	$	1,000.00	$	30,772.48

Notes:

_____

_____

_____

_____

43	$	52,547.60	$	1,000.00	$	34,949.73
44	$	57,802.36	$	1,000.00	$	39,544.70
45	$	63,582.59	$	1,000.00	$	44,599.17
46	$	69,940.85	$	1,000.00	$	50,159.09
47	$	76,934.94	$	1,000.00	$	56,275.00
48	$	84,628.43	$	1,000.00	$	63,002.50
49	$	93,091.27	$	1,000.00	$	70,402.75
50	$	102,400.40	$	1,000.00	$	78,543.02
51	$	112,640.44	$	1,000.00	$	87,497.33
52	$	123,904.48	$	1,000.00	$	97,347.06
53	$	136,294.93	$	1,000.00	$	108,181.77
54	$	149,924.43	$	1,000.00	$	120,099.94
55	$	164,916.87	$	1,000.00	$	133,209.94
56	$	181,408.56	$	1,000.00	$	147,630.93
57	$	199,549.41	$	1,000.00	$	163,494.02
58	$	219,504.35	$	1,000.00	$	180,943.42
59	$	241,454.79	$	1,000.00	$	200,137.77
60	$	265,600.27	$	1,000.00	$	221,251.54
61	$	292,160.29	$	1,000.00	$	244,476.70
62	$	321,376.32	$	1,000.00	$	270,024.37
63	$	353,513.96	$	1,000.00	$	298,126.81
64	$	388,865.35	$	1,000.00	$	329,039.49
65	$	427,751.89	$	1,000.00	$	363,043.43
Total	**$8,000.00**	**$ 427,751.89**	**$ 37,000.00**	**$ 363,043.43**		

Notes:

_____

_____

_____

_____

Eddie's total investment: $8,000. Result at age 65: $427,751.89
Pete's total investment: $37,000. Result at age 65: $363,843.43

The cost of waiting to build your financial future is too great! You must begin today!

Now, we need to change the way we think about money. To do this, we need to think like the rich, not the poor. That's what chapter five is all about. It's time to start thinking **RICH!**

Notes:

_____

_____

_____

_____

CHAPTER FIVE

THE DIFFERENCE BETWEEN
BROKE PEOPLE AND FREE PEOPLE

The Deceitfulness of Wealth

Have you ever been driving down the road and driven through a wealthy neighborhood? You see homes that look more like palaces. You see driveways with SUVs, Cadillacs and Mercedes and you wonder, "What do these people do for a living?"

It was 1986 and Connie and I moved our young family into, what was for us, a very well-to-do neighborhood. I remember how hard we struggled for the first two years just to make the house payments. I would walk around the neighborhood, rather proud of myself for achieving a nice level of success (not realizing what a dummy I actually was). My income was closing in on six figures and life seemed good.

One of the first people we met in the neighborhood was Craig and Donna. They since have become among our dearest friends. Craig was a doctor and the Director of Emergency at a local area hospital. Yep! I was in the right neighborhood. Later, I met another neighbor. He worked on the assembly line at Chrysler. I thought, *the assembly line!?* Another neighbor worked as a plumber! Wait a minute, I thought.

Notes:

_____

_____

_____

_____

These are common labor jobs. How can they afford a home in this neighborhood? It was then I began to realize that career position is not the key to financial freedom! I know people with some very prestigious career positions who are totally broke and in debt. Many people live in big fancy homes, yet can't afford to furnish them. Some people drive very nice automobiles but have trouble coming up with the gas money. *It's not how much you make, where you live, or the position or career you hold, it's all about what you do with what you get.*

The Answer is Not More Earned Income!

When I was making $60,000 per year, I remember thinking "If only I could earn another $15,000 per year, I'd be all set." Then when I hit $75,000 per year, it was "If only I could earn $100,000, then $150,000, then $200,000 and on and on. Where does it end? You see I was making the greatest mistake of all. I believed more income would solve my problems! So, I became obsessed with how could I make more money. I stressed out my life! My marriage was hurting; my time with my children Kelly and Kris was hurting; my employees and customers were all sensing my stress and frustration! All I wanted was financial freedom. I falsely believed the answer was more income. I have since found that the answer lies not in how much money I earn, but what I do with the money I earn.

Obtaining Wealth

Many people believe the lottery is the answer to their future. They see someone on TV who just won 10 million dollars and think, they are set for life. The question is, are you willing to depend on your odds of

Notes:

_____

_____

_____

_____

winning the lottery? Have you ever heard the stories of how many lottery winners are broke again, 10 years later?

Another way to obtain wealth is to inherit it. Maybe you have a rich parent, aunt or uncle? That's great! But what you do with your inheritance is the key! If you don't know what to do with the money, you could quickly lose it all. Remember, solid financial habits are critical to your financial success. If you don't do the right things with a little, you'll never do the right things when you have a lot.

If you never win the lottery and if you don't have any rich relatives to inherit from, then that leaves you your job and the money your boss decides to pay you. How many of you believe your job is the key to you becoming financially free? I doubt it. However, the money you earn from your job and what you do with it, is the beginning of your financial freedom plan.

Focus More On Using The Money You Earn To Build Assets. *NOT On More EARNED Income!*

One of the greatest books I have ever read is Rich Dad, Poor Dad by Robert Kiyosaki. I strongly recommend it. In it Kiyosaki focuses on what the rich do that the poor don't.

To make his point, Kiyosaki uses a simplified but very understandable income statement and balance sheet.

Notes:

_____

_____

_____

_____

The Income Statement

The Income Statement only has two parts, income and expenses.

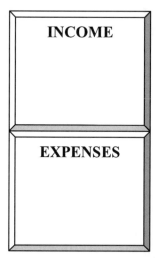

Income is anything that would bring "IN" money. It can be earned income, what you get from your job or work. It can be dividends off investments like a stock portfolio or mutual funds. It can also be interest income from investments or bank accounts. Finally, it can be passive income off of investments like real estate.

While income represents incoming money, expenses represent the outflow of money. Expenses are such bills as taxes, rent or mortgage, food, entertainment, clothing, gas, electric and so on.

Notes:

_____

_____

_____

_____

So, your income statement might look something like this:

INCOME
Paycheck
Dividends
Interest income
Real estate

EXPENSES
taxes,
rent or mortgage,
food, entertainment,
clothing, gas,
etc.

Notes:

_____

_____

_____

The Balance Sheet

The balance sheet also only has two parts. You may have guessed it. They are Assets and Liabilities.

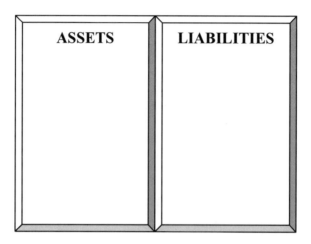

Robert Kiyosaki says an asset is anything that puts money in your pocket. A liability is anything that takes money out of your pocket. Assets can be stocks, bonds, real estate, notes or rare collectibles. Examples of liabilities are mortgages, consumer loans and credit card debt.

Notes:

_____

_____

_____

_____

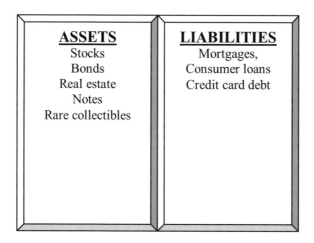

ASSETS	LIABILITIES
Stocks	Mortgages,
Bonds	Consumer loans
Real estate	Credit card debt
Notes	
Rare collectibles	

In simple terms, a person who is broke, in debt and financially poor uses his income to buy liabilities. A financially successful person uses his income to buy assets. It's that simple!

What The Poor Do

Most of us begin life with a job that doesn't pay the greatest. If we come out of high school and don't go to college, we believe that we are somehow restricted from making more because of our lack of education. Therefore, we never believe we will make a significant income and the only way we can ever hope to have some of the nicer things in life is to put them on a payment plan. While it's true a college education would make more "earned" income possible, earned income is not the key to your financial freedom. The poor don't live their life based on a net worth statement or balance sheet. Rather, they live on how much can

Notes:

_____

_____

_____

_____

they afford to pay every month. Therefore, a poor person will build up liabilities that demand more and more of his income and that makes putting anything in the asset column virtually impossible. When this happens, a poor person begins to believe the only answer to a better future is more earned income. However, the more earned income you get, the more debt you acquire. Why? Because now you believe you can afford more monthly payments. A poor person's statements would like this, based on income:

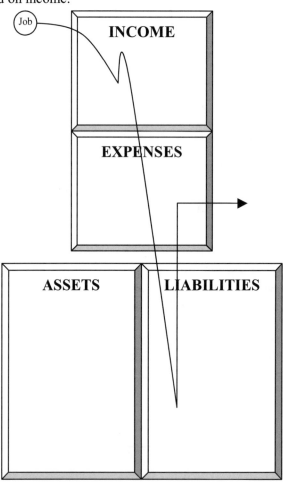

While a college education will get you more earned income, remember, it's what you do with what you get. I know many college graduates who are broke and in debt up to their eyeballs!

What The Rich Do

The rich are rich because they did something different with their income. Regardless of job or position, a rich person constantly looks for ways to use income to buy assets. Why? Assets produce more income! More income allows you to buy more assets. This way, you begin a cycle that never ends. The bigger your assets get, the faster your income grows. The faster your income grows, the bigger your assets get.

A person who finds ways to direct income to the asset column controls his own destiny. No longer do you have to depend on your boss to provide you hope of a better future. No longer do you have to depend on him for a pay raise to have a better future. Now, you control your financial destiny, not your boss! Each time you want more income, simply use some of your income to buy another asset that produces cash flow.

Notes:

_____

_____

_____

_____

This then is how the statements of a rich person look, based on income:

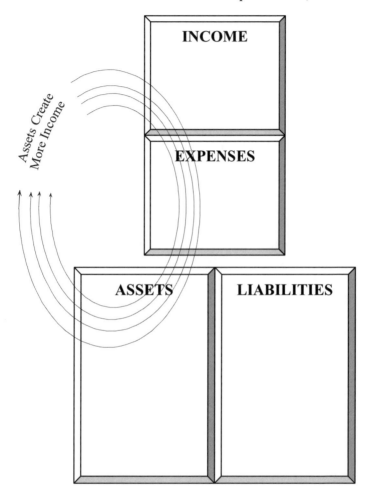

Notes:

_____

_____

_____

_____

The statements would look like this if you took a snapshot:

Poor

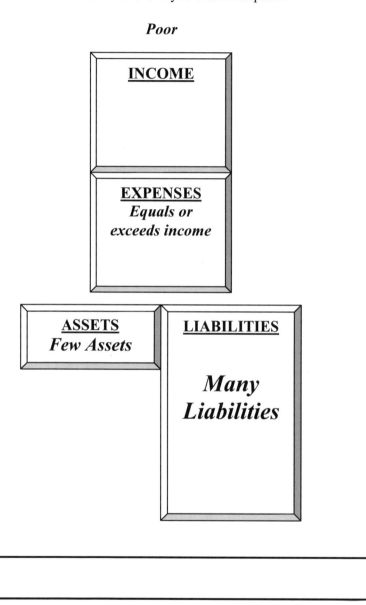

Notes:

_____

_____

_____

_____

Rich

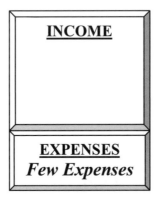

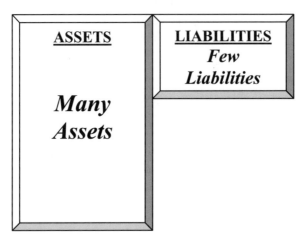

Notes:

_____

_____

_____

_____

Why do the rich persons statements look like this? Because they are a doctor, lawyer or movie-star? NO! I know many of these people who are broke! It's because of what they did with their income! Their assets are getting larger and the bigger they get, the more added income they produce to allow the rich to invest in more assets.

Robert Kiyosaki gives a great illustration of why the middle class struggles.

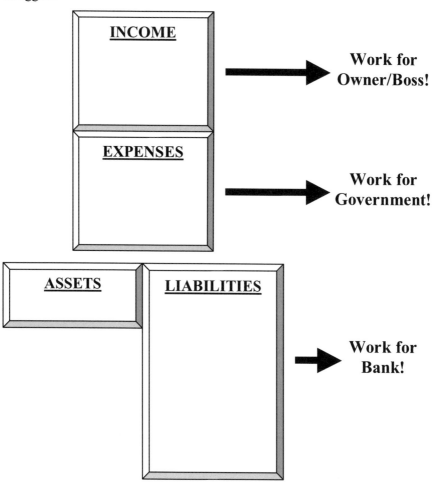

When you only generate earned income, than you work for your boss. The first thing taken out is taxes at a rate of 30 to 50% of our earned income. So our expenses show we work for the government. Finally, by accumulating so much debt, whom do you work for? The bank! You see, you work for everyone, except yourself and your family.

KEY:

Income buys assets. Assets buy homes, cars and boats!

RULE:

Once something goes into the asset column, it never comes out!

Probably, the number one reason for someone never building an investment portfolio is not being able to keep your hands off of it.

At my seminars, I am constantly bombarded by questions such as "Well, my wife and I want a new kitchen. So if we have the money sitting in our investment portfolio, wouldn't it make sense to use that rather than going in debt?" While I agree it's not a good idea to go in debt, I do not agree with using your investment portfolio to get the kitchen.
Ask yourself, if you didn't have an investment portfolio and wanted a new kitchen, how would you get it? Your first response was probably to charge it or borrow the money. *How about the idea of saving the extra money on top of your monthly investment amount?* If your answer is I can't afford to do that, then you shouldn't be getting a new kitchen! "But, Curt, I don't have the extra cash flow to save for a new kitchen!" How were you planning on making the payments if you borrowed the

Notes:

_____

_____

_____

_____

money? The same thing goes for anything you need. The minute you use your investment portfolio as you would a savings account, *you lose!*

As your assets get bigger, you can decide to use "some" of the earnings for that year to buy or purchase something of need. The key word in case you missed it was "SOME."

Let me give you an example: Let's say you had built your investment portfolio to a balance of $100,000. We will also assume you earned 8% in the last year on your account, or $8,000, and now have a balance of $108,000. Suppose you needed a new washer and dryer that would cost about $1,000.00. Since your asset grew by $8,000 it would be permissible to use $1,000 of the growth to buy the necessity. Note the emphasis on necessity! If it is a want but not a need, take the time to save the money and then buy it. However, if it is a need or necessity, rather than borrow the money, you can use **some** of the **growth** in your account **only.**

Obviously, if you make a habit of spending your growth, then you will never reach financial freedom. Be very careful then to never use all of your growth and only use part of it if it's an emergency. However, under NO circumstance, do you touch the principal balance from the previous year in your account.

As we head into chapter 6, we'll look at more ideas on getting control of your money rather than your money having control of you!

Notes:

_____

_____

_____

_____

CHAPTER SIX

GETTING CONTROL OF YOUR MONEY

One of the greatest and most memorable days for most of us is the day we graduate from high school and/or college. I remember my last semester of college. I was riding a bus back to school from my part-time job. The bus stopped at a traffic light and a car pulled up beside us. The driver was wearing a suit and all I could remember was staring out the window at him and saying, "Wow, he has a job!" I was so excited to be graduating in about four months that I found it hard to study and my GPA dropped from about a 3.5 to a 3.1 that semester.

Well, graduation day finally arrives. We are now ready to take on the world and begin our climb to the top. We find a job and realize on our first payday, "I'm Rich!" It doesn't matter what the salary. It's most likely, more money than we have ever made in our entire life!

It's so much money, now we have to figure out what to do with it. I know what I did. I Blew It! I was so sick and tired of being a broke college student, I just blew every last cent of that check!

Once we go totally spend one, two, three or maybe even four paychecks, the thrill of being out of school, working and having money, begins to wear off. And worse yet, we begin to realize that in the real world, this huge amount of money we were "raking in" suddenly seems very, very small. We must now begin to mature and figure out how to "budget"

Notes:

_____

_____

_____

_____

(*ugh!* What a nasty and ugly word!) our cash flow. Since we've never done this before, how do we begin?

Think back to your school days. You know, the days where you had those classes that taught you all about money. Stuff like, how to balance a checkbook. How about the class in school on laying out a family budget? Maybe it was a class on investing or the stock market. Or, better yet, what the rich do that the poor don't! Doesn't ring a bell? That's probably because you never had a class on these subjects. Like every other high school grad, you came out of school having learned all about English, math, science, reading, writing and even Christopher Columbus. However, you most likely learned absolutely nothing about handling money.

I am a major advocate of a proper education. However, one that doesn't teach one lesson on how to manage money or even the foundational principles of investing is, in this writer's opinion, a major omission in our educational system.

I believe every school in America should be providing classes on financial subjects. Teaching:

- Balancing a checkbook
- Investing for retirement
- The miracle of compounding interest
- Selecting a home mortgage
- How to fill out a basic tax form

If you're really fortunate, you may have been taught "properly" by your mother or father all about money. Although, if that were the case, I

Notes:

_____

_____

_____

_____

doubt you'd be reading this book! As a matter of fact, the odds are your parents had to learn by trial and error, and possibly are still learning and may not be the best teachers of the subject. In Chapter 4, we covered "Symptoms Of Personal Financial Problems," and we also looked at "12 Steps To Get Out Of Debt". Now, let's look at how to really get control of our cash flow.

Getting Control

Everywhere you turn, there are financial books teaching the need to create a budget. Yet, very few people would ever say to you that they became "financially free" as a result of having a budget. So why do so many books teach it as paramount to financial freedom? I believe it's because their authors have never tried to live on a budget themselves!

In his book, "Ordinary People, Extraordinary Wealth", Ric Edelman speaks of what his financially successful clients do concerning budgeting.

My clients consider budgeting to be a complete waste of time, evidenced by the fact that only 6% have and follow a budget. And don't think that this is only because my clients are rich, and that rich people don't need to follow a budget, because only 21% of my clients say that they ever had a budget – and even when they had it, only 24% strictly followed it. So if you've been struggling with a budget, and feeling guilty for not following it closely, you can stop – both the budgeting and feeling guilty!

On the other hand, there's widespread agreement that tracking expenses is worthwhile, because 76% of my clients say they do it. This is an important distinction because there's a big difference between budgeting

Notes:

_____

_____

_____

_____

and tracking expenses. The former is a promise of how you will spend your money; the latter reflects how you actually do spend it. And while budgeters often spend more than they had earlier promised themselves – creating such problems as falling into debt – trackers keep themselves well on track for their goals."

Does this mean we should not have any plan at all for our money? Not really. I just believe it should be far simpler to follow, and evolve more around a "cash system."

Here's how it works. Take a moment and categorize all of your spending over the last three months, not counting cash purchases. Most people only pay cash when it is a smaller amount. Larger purchases are usually done with a check or credit card. Therefore, get each of your credit card statements for the last three months. Also, get out your checkbook ledger. (This is called tracking by the way)

Grab a notepad and as you review each expense, create a category for it. Some examples:

- Auto expenses
- Groceries
- Clothing
- Utilities
- Mortgage or rent payment

This can be made far simpler by using computer software like "Quicken" or "Managing Your Money." If you will track your expenses by logging them on the computer each month, it becomes very easy to review and

Notes:

_____

_____

_____

_____

see where your money is going. However, if a computer is not available to you, the ole note pad will certainly do the trick.

Now, list each payment made in each category as you created them. Auto expenses might include car payment(s), oil changes and repairs. Once all expenditures are noted, add up all payments made in each category. Then total all the categories.

The only thing left to add is your 10% investment (minimum) that you will pay to yourself each payday. This cannot be part of your budgeted amount. Your investment is made first, before anything is allocated to any part of a cash management plan. It must come off the top!

Whatever is left goes into your pocket as cash. This is the money you use to purchase items not paid for by your checkbook. Things like gum, candy and burgers. The small miscellaneous items usually purchased on a moments notice.

It is a good idea to track these expenses for at least one month. You would be amazed how much money you're spending in areas you never thought about. By eliminating some of these areas, you leave more cash in your pocket for things that may be more important.

Notes:

_____

_____

_____

How Do You Make Sure You Don't Cheat Yourself On Your Investment Plan Into The Asset Column?

The key to investing is to have it done automatically, so you never see the money. This can sometimes be accomplished through a company 401K or 403B Plan. By using this plan through your employer, when offered, you never see the money. Many of the people I counsel on their investments, who have $1,000,000 or more to invest, have done a large part of it through their company retirement plan.

If you don't have a company retirement plan, many employers will allow you to direct deposit into a bank or credit union. Simply instruct your employer to send 10% of each paycheck to the bank and then establish an automatic bank draft with the investment of your choice to automatically deduct that amount from your bank account into your investment account. If your employer offers nothing in this regard to help, you can still do it by physically depositing the 10% yourself into an account set up just for your investment transfers.

It is important that your automatic investment each payday is not added to either account "A" or "B" (more on this in a minute). If it is part of the budget, and you get tight on money one month, you will "attack" your only key to financial freedom. You'll take the money intended for investments saying, "We'll just have to start investing again next month." The only problem is, you've now started a cycle or habit that can become impossible to break. You have short-circuited the entire plan for your financial freedom.

Once all your categories are complete, this now becomes the extent of your budget!

Notes:

_____

_____

_____

_____

The next step is to open an additional checking account for your budgeted items. We'll call this new checking account, account (A). Each payday you deposit into the "Cash-flow" checkbook "A," enough to pay your bills for each category created above. As the bills come due, no worry, the money is there waiting. Simply pay the bill. After depositing the money necessary to meet your monthly obligations, the remaining money then goes into one of two places. It either goes into a second checking account, we'll call your "cash" account (B) that can be used for everything else, or, it goes into your pocket as cash!

Now, here's the key. When the money in account "B" is gone or the money in your pocket is gone, you're done spending until payday comes around again.

I remember when my wife Connie and I were deep in debt and totally overwhelmed by it all. I would come home from work, only to find my wife huddled in the corner of the sofa covered in tears. You see, like many days, she had just received about five phone calls from creditors demanding payment for back debt. Some hard lessons were learned in those times.

Earning More Money Is Not The Answer!

Once again, allow me to beat on this subject. The average person would say, "If I just had an extra $500.00 per month, it would solve all of my financial problems. That's the furthest thing from the truth! You see it is human nature to spend what we make.

Notes:

_____

_____

_____

_____

Have you ever noticed how much money you make today compared to five or 10 years ago? Yet, you feel just as strapped or broke as you did when you made far less earned income. Yes, inflation has something to do with it, but people as a whole are making far more money today then ever before. Earning more money is not the answer! While earning more money may be necessary in your case, remember the key is, It's what you do with what you get.

Remember, more money times bad habits still equals zero. More money times, good financial habits, equals financial freedom! Without learning this, those who are in debt while living on one income will almost always be in debt with two incomes. Having said that, those who wisely know what to do with the money they get, will almost always live just as well on one income as they did on two incomes. This can mean one parent staying home, if that's your desire.

So, what do we do, when account "A" is funded, but there's not enough money to support account "B?" We have to find ways to reduce our monthly overhead. This was covered in Chapter 4 when we found the extra money to pay off our debt and begin building our investments and net-worth. The financial freedom plan I outline in this book will not work if every month, you are spending more than you are earning. We must either reduce how much we spend or increase how much we earn coupled with doing the proper things with the extra money.

Don't Spend Tomorrow's Dollars On Today's Needs

One of the worst habits we can ever develop is the idea of spending money that we believe is coming in but haven't yet received.

Notes:

_____

_____

_____

_____

From the time I was 16 years old, my career was built in the radio broadcasting industry. In 1981, I took a job as general manager of a radio station in the St. Louis, Missouri area.

As Connie and I began searching for a home to raise our family in, we found the perfect house in Bellville, Illinois. The town is just a few miles east of the Mississippi River from St. Louis. Our home was far more than we could afford at the time, based on my starting salary. However, I told Connie not to worry, because within 6 months my income would be so much higher as the radio station gained in popularity. I was buying the house, not based on the income I could count on, rather on income "I believed" I would be making in the future.

Needless to say, things at the station did not go as planned. We were so strapped financially that we had no living room furniture, no dining room furniture, a table and some chairs in the kitchen and a love seat and TV in a 20 X 16 foot family room. We had no blinds or curtains on the windows on the first floor.

One day we were sitting in our kitchen eating dinner when a total stranger walked up on the deck in the backyard and leaned onto the sliding door with their hands over his eyes staring through our sliding glass doors at us. He thought the house was vacant!

Tips

I think one of the greatest commercials of recent times is by Southwest Airlines. Each ad has someone caught in a very embarrassing moment. Then you hear the line "want to get away?"

Notes:

_____

_____

_____

_____

Many people use the mall as the place they decide they would like to get away to. We use excuses like, it's soothing and it's relaxing. While walking a mall may accomplish this for some, the soothing and relaxing feeling is soon gone when the bills come in from unnecessary expenditures, all done while "relaxing." Have you ever wondered why malls were created in the first place? Retailers discovered, if the could get you inside, the odds of you spending something escalates dramatically.

Do not under any circumstance shop for entertainment. Wandering through malls and shopping centers usually produces unnecessary spending. It also breeds discontent to look at all the latest things we don't have, don't need and can't afford.

Grocery stores are also extremely high tech and well thought out. Grocery retailers are constantly fine tuning their marketing to get you to spend more than you intended to when you entered their "web" oh…sorry, front doors. Below, are some procedures to keep in mind when the need to go grocery shopping arises.

Grocery Shopping Procedures

Compare Stores
There can be a big difference
Check advertisements for sales
Use coupons
$10 per week savings results in $520 per year into your freedom plan.
Have a budget for food
It helps you be more conscious when shopping

Notes:

_____

_____

_____

_____

Make a list and stick to it
This prevents the, "u-m-m-m-m that looks good."
Eat before shopping
When you shop hungry, you will always spend more money.
Check bottom shelves
This is where the best deals are sometimes hidden.
Understand unit pricing
Some packaging may look like the same size as another (cereal is the greatest example). However, when you look at unit pricing, it gives you are far better apple-to-apple comparison of the cost of a product.
Check no name brands
They can be just as good and tasty, and save money.
Take advantage of refunds
It's free money!

OK, we now have our easy-to-follow cash flow plan. We've allocated the amount to invest in our asset column each month. Now, let's learn more about money and how to invest it.

Notes:

_____

_____

_____

_____

CHAPTER SEVEN

MONEY, FINANCIAL FREEDOM AND INVESTING

As we now begin to talk about investing, I felt I would be remiss if I did not begin this chapter without some discussion on the subject of money itself.

It is important to remember there can be a distinct difference between financial freedom and being rich. Financially free people may not always be rich, although they usually tend to be. A rich person may not be financially free. Any person no matter what occupation or income level can be financially free. A bus driver can be financially free, just as a doctor and lawyer can be.

Financial freedom means your asset base is sufficient to generate the income needed to support your lifestyle, whether or not you choose to work for earned income. The lower your debt and income demands, the simpler it is to be financially free. I tie financial freedom more to happiness than the idea of being rich to happiness. Can you think of people you are familiar with who are rich? Maybe they are business people or famous movie stars or recording artist. A person can be rich but very unhappy. While I suppose a financially free person could be unhappy as well, I believe it is less likely. You see, financially free people have learned to control their spending and build their asset

Notes:

_____

_____

_____

_____

column through wise investing. They are now free in life to pursue whatever dreams they may have. Financially free people now have enough of an asset base and virtually no bad debt, they can live off their assets. I believe this leads to a more peaceful and happy life. It can lead to a life of less stress and more joy. Financial freedom is not tied to a level of income either. Financial freedom means doing what you want to with your life. Getting up when your body is rested. Going to bed when you're tired. Financial freedom is spending more time with family members or people you love and care about. It goes beyond how much money you have.

John D. Rockefeller, unquestionably one of the richest men of his day said; "The poorest man I know, is the man who has nothing but money."

John D. Rockefeller: "I have made many millions, but they have brought me no happiness."

W.H. Vanderbilt: "The care of $200,000,000 is enough to kill anyone. There is no pleasure in it."

John Jacob Astor: "I am the most miserable man in the world."

Henry Ford: " I was happier when I was doing a mechanics job."

Andrew Carnegie: "Millionaires seldom smile."

To be happy when we have a lot of money (which you can by following the principles of this book). You must learn to be happy now, no matter what your present circumstance may be. Remember the man on the road to a new town who saw an old man on the side of the road and asked him

Notes:

_____

_____

_____

_____

what the people were like in the new town? This is the same principle. Never forget, the best things in life tend to be free. The Bible says; "Whoever can be trusted with very little can also be trusted with much."[*] You can reverse it and apply that to your income. Whoever can't be trusted with $4,000 per month, certainly can't be trusted with $50,000 per month. Nor, contrary to what many may teach, does the Good Book tell us to stay away from worldly wealth. Rather, we must use it wisely and strategically.[**]

[*] Luke 16;10
[**] Luke 16:19

Investing

If I were to ask you what is the most important bill that you pay each month, what would it be? Is it your mortgage? Is it your auto payment? Stop for one moment and pick the bill you would think is the most important. Do you have it? The correct answer is to pay yourself!

Rule #1 is "PAY YOURSELF FIRST!" It's human nature to spend our entire disposable income and to rationalize all those expenditures as needs. The only way to make sure we are investing consistently is to do it automatically through some of the means discussed in chapter 6. The key is that the amount you invest must come right off the top. Never, I repeat, never, pay your bills and then try to invest what's left. Why? There's never anything left! At the writing of this chapter, I believe the market offers some great investment opportunities. I believe no matter what the economic outlook, no matter what the markets are doing, it is always a good time to begin investing. A little later in this chapter, I will share some ideas that prove this point. Whether the market is going up or down, you can always come out the winner. I'll show you how.

Notes:

_____

_____

_____

_____

The Miracle Of Compounding Interest

To begin, I want to take you on a magical journey through the miracles of compounding interest. Compounding interest can work both for you and against you (when you carry bad debt).

Many people have called compound interest the 8th wonder of the world (especially when it works for you rather than against you). Throughout this book, you will find many examples of compounding interest to help you understand this 8th wonder that will help set you financially free. Allow me to show you one example now. Assume you could invest just $83 per month at 10%. Check the amount invested against the actual balance of the account over time.

	Amount Invested	Balance
10 years	$ 9,960	$ 17,002
20 years	$19,920	$ 63,028
30 years	$29,880	$187,620
40 years	$39,840	$524,899

Many people believe that in order to truly be successful at investing, they must achieve the highest possible return on their investment. While gaining a high return is important, it is just as important to protect your investments from loss as much as possible.

Notes:

_____

_____

_____

_____

Which account would you rather have?

In account "A," you invest $10,000. The first year you earn an 80% return on your investment. The second year is a tough one and your account loses 50%.

In account "B," you invest the same $10,000 and receive 5% interest in each of the same two years.

Which one sounds like the best investment to you? At the end of two years, account "A" has a balance of $9,000. Account "B" has a balance of $11,025.

Let me give you another example (although this time I'm sure you'll be watching for the catch). Again, you have a choice between accounts "A" or "B." In both accounts, you invest $100,000. Account "A" pays you a 20% return in year one and then again in year two. Then the investment has an off year and loses 20% in year three. Finally, it pays another positive return in year four, again at 20%. Account "B" pays you only 10% per year. However, never loses money. It looks like this:

	Account "A"	Account "B"
Year 1	+20%	+10%
Year 2	+20%	+10%
Year 3	- 20%	+10%
Year 4	+20%	+10%
The result!	Account "A"	Account "B"
	$138,240	$146,410

Notes:

_____

_____

_____

_____

I think these ideas get the point across of the need to be a wise investor and the importance of protecting your investments as much as gaining a good return.

It is also believed that to begin investing, you must have a fair sum of money to invest, or it's not worth troubling yourself. When Connie and I started out as a young married couple, we were in our second year of marriage when I saw an ad on TV that caught my interest. I was in radio broadcasting at the time and saw this huge bull walking through a china shop and amazingly chose his path carefully enough so as to not disturb or destroy even one piece of china. I was so impressed, that I began to think that maybe I should call these "bullish" folks up and begin my journey to wealth. The only problem in my mind was that I only had about $2,000 to invest at the time. I figured I'd wait until I had at least $5,000 saved and then make the call. You guessed it! I never made the call (by the time I did figure this out, I was in the financial planning field and didn't need the bullish folks).

If you always wait until you've saved enough money to begin investing, you may never get there. Remember, when we are wise with a little, we can be trusted with much!

One of the greatest secrets to long-term wealth is to gather it one nut at a time.

Have you ever spotted squirrels hard at work? They are relentless in their task. They go about collecting food for the long winter months, storing them up to make sure they can survive the frigid winter. Your investment portfolio can begin the same way.

Notes:

_____

_____

_____

_____

Don't get me wrong. If you're fortunate enough to have some investments already started, continue to build upon that beginning. However, for those of you just getting started, it's all about accumulation.

The Bible says, "He who gathers money little by little, makes it grow." (Proverbs 13:11) It's the little investments that make all of the difference.

Let's look at an example of little by little vs. whenever we get a big chunk.

You've developed your "freedom plan" and have found, you can put an extra $200 per month toward debt and therefore also $200 per month is available to invest. We'll assume you invest this $200 each month into a growth mutual fund (more on this later) at an average rate of return of 10% for the next twenty years.

The other option would be to wait until we had enough to make a larger investment. So, we would save up the $200 per month for four years, at which time we would have $9,600. Then every four years, invest the $9,600 a total of five times over the next twenty years.

Plan #1: Invest $200/month. For 20 years.
Plan #2: Invest $9,600 every four years. (a total of five times) over the next 20 years.

In both cases, you would have invested the same amount of money, $48,000. Look at the results at the end of 20 years.
Plan #1 = $151,874 Plan #2 = $118,473

Notes:

_____

_____

_____

_____

You have an extra $33,401 more in your account. Why? Because you did it little by little and didn't wait until you had enough money to feel like now you're ready to invest.

The first key to investing then is using the miracle of compound interest coupled with saving little by little.

The second key to investing is TIME.

Remember the story of Eager Eddie and Procrastinator Pete from Chapter 4? That story illustrates as much as anything, the value of time.

To further illustrate, take a look at the chart below. This will give you another idea of the difference time can make and the reason to begin investing now.

Assuming you invest only $83 per month at 10% until age 65

Begin at age 55	**$ 17,002.13**
Begin at age 45	**$ 63,027.61**
Begin at age 35	**$187,620.50**
Begin at age 25	**$524,898.60**

Stop and think about it. $83 per month is only $19.30 per week (4.3 weeks per mo) or $2.76 per day! What do you spend on fast food every day? For less than the price of a combo, you're on your way to financial freedom!

Notes:

_____

_____

_____

_____

OK, OK, I'm sold, but where do I invest my money?

If you are over the age of 21, as I'm sure most everyone reading this book is, then the story of Pete and Eddie most likely made you a little frustrated to think of all the money you've lost toward your retirement due to less time. However, I want to encourage you again to remember, it's never, I repeat never, too late to begin.

Most people new to investing tend to look to look at investments that are either far too conservative or far too risky. The banks offer safety and their products are easy to understand. The only problem is their programs pay among the lowest rates of return. Depending on your age and time left until you desire to retire, this may be insufficient to help you achieve your financial goals.

This then causes us to look at the stock and bond markets to invest. However, we are usually fearful of the stock market, as we all have heard how people can lose money there. Our goal is to gain money into our asset column as fast as we can, yet to do it with the least amount of risk necessary to reach our goals.

The greatest reason for fear of the stock market is clear, we don't understand the stock market. What we don't understand, we tend to avoid. Unfortunately, the stock market is the proven winner over time for most investors. The other fact <u>we must fear</u> is the threat of inflation. Inflation has run lower in recent years; however, it can still destroy our dreams for the future. Take a look at the historical rates of return listed below and what inflation can do to each one.

Notes:

_____

_____

_____

1926 to 1999

	%	After tax %	After Tax/Inf/%
Large Cap Stks	11.3%	7.09%	3.99%
Small Cap Stks	12.6%	7.86%	4.76%
Corp. Bonds	5.6%	3.49%	.48%
Govt. Bonds	5.1%	3.18%	.08%
CD's / T-Bills	3.8%	2.37%	(.73%)loss

RESULT: Long-term money invested for five to 10 years or longer should be in equities within the markets. The only time this may not be the right decision is if you are already within five years of retirement. Then, the potential return is not worth the risk because you don't have enough of the most critical ingredient left, time.

Balance is important

I'm not sure why certain things that happen in our childhood seem to stick in our minds. They can be the simplest things as well. One thing that has stuck, and I'm glad it did, is a saying my father, Marvin, taught me. He said, "Son, in everything you do in life, let there be balance." If we drink alcohol, make sure there's balance. If we exercise, make sure there's balance. When we eat, make sure there's balance. When we work in a career, make sure there's balance between our career and family. I'm sure if you think about it, you will come up with some of your own ideas on balance.

In investing it also holds true, you must be balanced. From the year 2000 through 2002 and at the writing of this chapter maybe even 2003, the U.S. stock market has taken the greatest fall since 1929. I hope we have

Notes:

_____

_____

_____

_____

all learned some valuable lessons. Here's a template to go by, a rule of thumb that most financial planners go by.

Subtract your current age from 100. The result is how much of your investments should be market type of investments or investments that carry risk. The balance of your investments should be held in secure accounts that have little or no downside risk.

For example, a 25-year-old might have 75% of their investments at risk and only 25% in safer positions. A 40-year-old would be 60% at risk and 40% safe. A 65-year-old would have 35% at risk and 65% safe.

When invested in the stock market, you will always have cycles of good and bad times. Times when the economy looks good and investments in general are all heading up in value. The old saying what goes up must come down also seems to hold true. There will always be cycles of time when investment values will decline in the market. The younger you are, the longer you can wait for a declining investment value to rebound. The older you are, you tend to not be as patient; you don't have as many years to wait for the rebound, before you may begin to need your assets to live on. Therefore, the rule is the older you are the more the balance of your accounts should shift to safer investments.

I have worked with many retirees who, I believe, have far too much of their investments in risk positions. It is not unusual for someone to come into my office with an investment portfolio of over one and a half million to two million dollars, and have 80% or more of it at risk. Why does this happen? It's because that's what they are being sold by their stockbroker. With an investment portfolio of two million dollars, even conservatively, that would provide an income of $100,000 to $120,000

Notes:

_____

_____

_____

_____

per year. Why take the risk on losing potentially 40% of your entire account and jeopardizing your future and even present income needs? For that portion of our investments that we do invest in the stock market, there is a strategy to follow.

Always buy your clothes on sale when possible!

Are you a shopper? Do you have a person in your home who absolutely loves the thrill of the chase for a real good deal? If so, then make sure that person helps you buy all of your investments.

Let's say you're walking through the mall one day, and you happen to see the most beautiful outfit at your favorite apparel store. The only problem is it cost $250. Being the wise shopper that you are, you decide to keep a keen eye on it and wait until it goes on sale. The next week, you come by the same store again and see your outfit is no longer $250, rather, it went up to $275. You're shocked! This has never happened before! The next week it rises to $300. Would you buy it? NO! Why not? It would be ridiculous to buy an outfit that's going up in price! The smart thing would be to wait for it to go on sale and then buy it.

Buy Your Stocks The Same Way.

Why then do we do just the opposite in buying stocks? We see a stock at $20 and really like the company. However, we decide to watch it. It goes to $25, then to $30, then to $50. Before long, we can't stand watching it go up, so we buy it, at $52! Then what happens? The stock went up so fast, it became overvalued, so people began to sell shares and the price quickly went back down to $25 where it probably belongs.

Notes:

_____

_____

_____

_____

We need to take a lesson from the wise shoppers. When you see a company you really like, watch and wait for it to go on sale. Then, when it is undervalued, as long as you believe in the company, buy it and watch as the sale ends and the value once again begins to climb. Of course, to buy stocks, does require having a block of money to invest. So, how can I invest if I'm just starting out and only have $100 to $300 per month to invest?

Mutual Funds

One of the greatest investment vehicles ever created for the small investor was the mutual fund. Mutual funds make it possible for the little guy to invest on a regular basis in the future of our economy. It's a way to buy stock, bond, real estate, gold and other related investments on a monthly basis or for a minimal one-time investment.

What is a mutual fund? Let's say you and nine of your friends got together and decided to begin investing in some stocks. However, none of you had any money to speak of but believed you could save about $167 per month, or $2,000 per year each. That would mean each month the 10 of you would be investing $1,670 or about $20,000 per year. This amount would certainly be enough to buy some stock. So alone, you couldn't do it, but together you can generate enough money.

The next problem is that you need someone who is smart and understands the stock market. Someone who will help the ten of you decide what to invest in. So you run out and find a person who understands the market and has a history of selecting good stocks that generally go up in value. However, this person says to you that they

Notes:

_____

_____

_____

_____

can't afford the time to help you without being paid. So you and your friends decide to give this person 5% of what you invest each month in exchange for his/her help in investing your money.

We just described in simple terms what a mutual fund is. A company will form a fund and hire a manager to make the investment decisions. Then they market their fund to the public. Anyone can invest a small some of money either monthly or one time, and their manager, for a fee or percentage. Will do the investing for you.

For new investors especially, or those without much time to study, this is the ideal investment vehicle. Let me warn you, if you do not have a lot of time to learn and understand investing in the markets. Do not attempt it without the help of a professional or using mutual funds.

I recommend the best starting point is to look at index funds. These are mutual funds that usually have very low fees because the only thing they have to do is by the stocks of the companies on that exchange. A great example is a Dow Jones Index fund. The Dow is only made up of 30 stocks out of thousands on the market. Yet, owning an equal percentage of these 30 companies has consistently outperformed most every mutual fund manager picking stocks on his own. Therefore, seek out an index fund and begin your investing there. You will find some of these funds available through many companies. I have listed a partial listing of some of the most popular fund companies in the back of the book under appendix "A" complete with 800 numbers for you to call for a prospectus and more information.

If you have the time and you're a self-starter, you can call these companies direct and begin investing. If you like having the advice of a

Notes:
_____

_____

_____

_____

professional, I recommend you seek one out through a friend or family member. Using a financial planner through a referral is always the best way to find one. This way, you know that at least your friend is happy with their service. You still must ask questions and do some research. However, this is far better than picking one out of the phone book that you don't have a clue what there experience or knowledge is like or anything about their integrity. I will talk more about picking a financial advisor in a later chapter.

Mutual Fund Fees

Fund managers have to be paid for selecting the stocks in the fund you own a piece of. How are they paid? Furthermore, if you use a financial planner or stockbroker, how are they paid for helping you?

First, let's talk about the fund manager. Each mutual fund has annual fees associated with it. They can vary greatly, and that is why you want to read "at least" the section of the prospectus on the fund that talks about fees. I have found them charging from a low of .20% ($1/5^{th}$ of a percent) to as high as 3% per year or higher of the balance of your account. I believe any fund charging between .60% and 1.25% is reasonable. Obviously, however, the lower the fees the better, as long as you are sure it is the right fund for you.

If you have $10,000 in a mutual fund and the fee is 1% to the manager, then you are paying $100 for that year to the manager. You never see the fee, nor are you billed for it. It comes right off the top. If the fund says you earned 12% that year, they actually earned 13% and paid you 12%.

Notes:

_____

_____

_____

_____

Some (usually non-professionals) will tell you that the lower the fee the better. While this could be true, it isn't always the case! Always make sure to base your investment decision first on the ability of the manager and their past performance, then on the size of the fee. Manager "A" may only charge you ½ %, but your net return is 8%. Manager "B" may charge you 1.25%, but your net return after fees is 12%. I think you get the idea.

There are three ways that the financial advisor usually gets paid. That's through three types of shares.

"A" Shares: This is a fee that comes right off the top of your investment. They can range in size, but traditionally they would be around 5%. Don't confuse these costs with management fees. They are over and above management fees. Therefore, if you invested $1,000, your opening balance would be $950. The other $50 went to the Financial Advisor who recommended the fund to you in the form of a commission.
I hope you won't be too concerned over this. If you are capable of doing everything on your own, that's great! However, if you feel your knowledge is insufficient to venture out on your own, please don't begrudge a professional advisor for providing for his family by giving you knowledgeable advice. Your Financial Advisor could save you a tremendous amount of heartache and loss of money by helping you plan properly for your financial goals.

"A" shares usually come with lower management fees than "B" shares. If an "A" share charges 5% to get in, it may have an annual management fee of .60%. Let's compare "B" shares.

Notes:

_____

_____

_____

_____

"B" shares: When you purchase "B" shares, there is no upfront sales charge or commission. If you invest $1,000, your full $1,000 goes to work for you. What's the catch? Early withdrawal charges are assessed if you liquidate your account prior to the term agreed upon.

Most "B" shares have a five-year commitment to the fund. If you leave in the fund in the first year, you would pay a surrender charge (S/C) of 5% of the value of your investment. Each year, the charge would then drop by one percent. If you leave in year four, your S/C would be 4%, year three your S/C would be 3% down to at the end of five years, there would no longer be any fees.

The second factor is that "B" shares charge a higher management fee in the first five years than "A" shares in the same fund would charge. Once the five years is over, the "B" shares automatically convert to "A" shares again. Where as "A" shares may charge a management fee of .60%, a "B" share might charge 1.25%

"C" shares: These shares may have no upfront charges and no S/C's, or could come with a one year S/C of 1%. They can even have a lower management fee. What you will find with these shares are that most financial advisors won't even offer them unless they are charging you a separate fee or hourly rate for their time. Again, please don't begrudge a professional financial advisor for charging for their services and expertise.

No-load funds: No-Loads have no upfront fees no S/C's and usually carry lower management fees. Again, if you want professional advice, be willing to pay for it. If you can venture out on your own, a no-load fund may be the way to go. Be careful not to ignore "A" and "B" shares,

Notes:

_____

_____

_____

_____

even if you are doing your own planning. It is possible for a "A" or "B" to outperform a "C," even after the charges and fees.

Timing the market

After all my years of investing and being in the market, I have found trying to time when to buy and when to sell stocks is the most difficult thing to do. I tried timing services. I didn't find them to work any better than most mutual funds and they came with higher fees.

I bought all of the top software on the market to try graphing and using technical indicators in hopes of finding the perfect system that would teach me when to buy and when to sell. While studying fundamental and technical analysis did help me make some better decisions, I found the time commitment to learning them and then following the various stocks I was tracking was asking too much.

I like most people had a job/career and family. Between Little League sports, parent teacher meetings and family time, it's not too easy to find the extra hour or two to constantly review and follow your investments and do the research necessary.

Remember, the importance of balance.   When I was researching fundamentals and viewing all of the technical graphs, I found my family life was falling out of balance. While I still like to look at the technical indicators for confirmation, I have found I am much happier when I can focus on my family, my business and my seminars and leave the detailed decisions to other professionals where that 's what they do best.

Notes:

_____

_____

_____

_____

Whenever most people try to time when to get in and when to get out of the market, they usually end up losing more than they get. They end up selling when they should be buying and buying when they should be selling. I liken it to gambling, in that you never truly know when to pull your money and walk. No matter what anyone may tell you, all investors are guessing. Some with more educated guesses than others, however, they are all guessing.

So then, when should you invest? The answer is all of the time. It's called Dollar Cost Averaging.

Dollar Cost Averaging

Dollar Cost Averaging (DCA) is a tried and true method for investing in higher risk investments. The idea is that if you invest the same amount of money on a predetermined basis (usually monthly). You can't really lose in the beginning.

Take a look at the chart below:

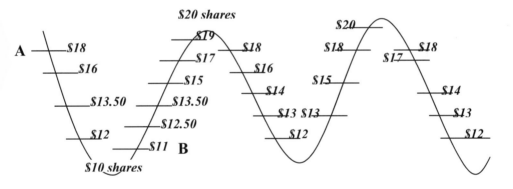

Notes:

_____

_____

_____

_____

This chart represents the market cycling and going up and down over a period of time. Each short horizontal line represents a point that you would have purchased some shares, the price you would have paid for the shares and how many shares your dollars would have bought based on the stock price.

First, let's say your first purchase was at point "A" on the chart. As you can see, each month for the next six months, the market went down. You WIN! How can you win when the market is going down? The name of the game in market investing is to buy low and sell high. For the first six months, that's exactly what you are doing. You're buying your stock on sale! You are accumulating far more shares each time you buy, as the price of the stock has gone down and made the shares cheaper. Thus you get more for your money. You see, in the beginning, you actually want the market to fall. The name of the game is "how many shares do I own. Then when the market begins to go back up (as it always has) at point "B" what happens to the value of all of those shares you bought on sale? They go up in value and you are making money!

You may say "shouldn't I stop buying the shares as they go up? If you can tell me for sure they are going up and you know each time the market will go up and each time it will go down, then I guess that would be a good idea. However, since you most likely don't know where the market is going next, it is better to just follow the DCA system of investing and the averages will work in your favor (see the average price per share in chart).

In the next chapter we will look at what I consider one of the most underrated investments in America. There are plenty of ways to reach

Notes:

_____

_____

_____

_____

our goal. The next investment has many additional options and features. Wait until you see it!

Notes:

_____

_____

_____

_____

CHAPTER EIGHT

INVESTING IN THE MOST UNDERRATED, INVESTMENT...ANNUITIES!

Many people don't even think about investing in annuities for two primary reasons. First, they don't quite understand them. All they have heard are some rumors from the '60's and '70's that unfortunately still hang around today (but are unfounded). Rumors that say annuities aren't very good, because you forfeit all of your investment in exchange for an income you will never outlive. While this was true 20+ years ago, and can still be an option today, in the early 80's the insurance industry (which offers annuities) made major changes that have made them excellent investment vehicles. I believe annuities, to some degree, should be in everyone's portfolio.

The second reason many people overlook the opportunity of investing in annuities, is that their stockbroker doesn't like them and will seldom if ever recommend them. Why? Annuities are intended to be long-term investment vehicles. Usually, once you purchase one, the term of investment will be from three to 10 years. Annuities pay the selling representative a commission. However, the commission comes from the company, not out of your pocket or investment. Because annuities pay a one-time commission to the selling representative and are longer-term investments, this means less commission for a broker over a period of time, than if he were constantly trading your investment.

Notes:

_____

_____

_____

_____

Stock Brokers like to invest your money in a way that allows them to trade it regularly. The reason for this is that each time they move your money, they are paid a commission when they sell the investment you're leaving and they make another commission on the one your buying. I'm not saying they would trade your account just for the sake of a commission. However, there is far more commission to be made by trading your account over the long haul.

While I wouldn't recommend annuities by themselves, they can add a tremendous way to diversify and balance your investment portfolio.

How Do Annuities Work?

You can get an annuity for just about any investment plan you would like. The three main types of annuities are:

Fixed:	Like a bank CD only from an insurance company.
Variable:	Mutual funds with an extra bonus.
Equity Index:	Returns tied to the market with no downside risk.

First, some background information. Annuities are tax-deferred investments. This means, you do not have to claim your interest or dividend yields each year on your tax return while your investment remains inside the account. This is a major feature, and one that is over-looked by many. When I share the variable annuity, I'll show you just how powerful this feature is. Because of the tax-deferred feature, those over the age of 59 1/2 should only use annuities for retirement investments and long-term investments. Should you pull your investment out of the annuity markets prior to age 59 ½, you may be

Notes:

_____

_____

_____

_____

subject to a governmental penalty of 10% for early withdrawal, much like an IRA.

However, annuities do not have a mandatory required distribution at age 70 ½ like the IRA's and 401-K's. This means that money could be invested, never needed and therefore, the owners would never claim or pay income tax on this investment, again while it is in the account. It's a great spot to put retirement money for when you need it down the road. However, if you don't need it, you don't pay taxes. This way, all of your earnings are left in the account and create almost a double compounding. You now not only earn your interest, you also earn interest on the money that would have gone to Uncle Sam as tax. Let's get into each form of annuity.

Fixed Annuity:

When you go to your bank and make a time deposit, you are most likely buying a Certificate of Deposit (CD). These are guaranteed accounts with virtually no risk. You would receive a flat interest rate of say 3%. This rate is guaranteed for the term of the CD you choose. The major drawbacks of CD's are a lower rate of return and the fact you must pay taxes each year on any interest that you earned. Certificate Of Deposits are guaranteed by the Federal Deposit Insurance Corporation, FDIC, for $100,000.

A fixed annuity is similar to a CD; only, it is a time deposit issued by an insurance company. Even though an insurance company issues it, depending on the annuity it is an investment not tied to insurance.

Notes:

_____

_____

_____

The first thing people tend to ask is, is an annuity insured like bank money? Yes and no. The issuing company guarantees the annuity. However, in reality, should an insurance company ever go bankrupt, another usually larger company, that would honor all investor deposits and guarantee them, would buy out their assets and honor all investor claims. There has never been a time that I am aware of where an investor lost their investment with an insurance company.

Let me ask you this question. Who insures your car? Who insures your home, your life, your disability and your health? Does it make sense, that if you trust them with all of your most important possessions, you could trust them with an investment? In my 20 years of experience, I have personally never seen a time where you couldn't find a fixed annuity that didn't offer better yields than a CD.

Variable Annuity:

Earlier, we talked about mutual funds and what they are. Variable annuities are mutual funds with one difference. In a regular mutual fund, you must claim and pay tax on all dividends (kind of like interest) that you earn each year. Plus, if you sell your fund for a profit, you would also have to claim and pay tax on your capital gains. This happens whenever you sell a stock or a fund for a higher price than what you paid for it.

In a variable annuity, you do not have to claim any dividends or capital gains while the money is in the account. There is no required time you must pull the money out. Because it is tax-deferred, you have no taxes to pay on the internal buildup. To further illustrate the value of tax-deferral, look at the following chart:

Notes:

_____

_____

_____

_____

Taxable vs. Tax-Deferred
Assumes 10% Rate of Return

Annual Investment: $3,000

Year	Taxable	Tax-Deferred
1	$ 3,201.00	$ 3,300.00
2	$ 6,616.47	$ 6,930.00
3	$ 10,260.77	$ 10,923.00
4	$ 14,149.24	$ 15,315.30
5	$ 18,298.24	$ 20,146.83
6	$ 22,725.22	$ 25,461.51
7	$ 27,448.81	$ 31,307.66
8	$ 32,488.88	$ 37,738.43
9	$ 37,866.64	$ 44,812.27
10	$ 43,604.70	$ 52,593.50
11	$ 49,727.22	$ 61,152.85
12	$ 56,259.94	$ 70,568.14
13	$ 63,230.36	$ 80,924.95
14	$ 70,667.79	$ 92,317.45
15	$ 78,603.53	$ 104,849.19
16	$ 87,070.97	$ 118,634.11
17	$ 96,105.73	$ 133,797.52
18	$ 105,745.81	$ 150,477.27
19	$ 116,031.78	$ 168,825.00
20	$ 127,006.91	$ 189,007.50
21	$ 138,717.37	$ 211,208.25
22	$ 151,212.44	$ 235,629.07

Notes:

_____

_____

_____

_____

23	$	164,544.67	$ 262,491.98
24	$	178,770.16	$ 292,041.18
25	$	**193,948.76**	$ **324,545.30**

Monthly income in year 25 $ 11,636.93 $ 19,472.72
at 6%:

What's the difference if I pay tax now or later?
* 33% in taxes
     Cash out year 25: $ 193,948.76 $ 242,195.35

As you can see, tax-deferral on your long-term retirement money is extremely beneficial to your end result. I have had some people ask in my seminars, what's the difference if you pay tax on the money now, or later when you need it in retirement? Don't you still end up with the same amount of money? The answer is a big NO WAY!

First, should you want to draw an income from your assets in the chart above, would you rather draw an income off of $286,244 or off $698,993? True, either way, you will pay income tax on what you draw, but give me a break! This is what I call a no brainer for retirement dollars!

Variable's work very similar to mutual funds, in that you can make monthly contributions. In the next chapter on retirement, I will speak more on the best ways to use annuities and some of their additional benefits.

Notes:

_____

_____

_____

_____

Variable annuities can have higher management fees than a regular mutual fund. A reasonable fee for a Variable Annuity is about 1.35%. While this fee is most likely higher than a traditional mutual fund, some people may feel it worth it.

First, you have the benefit of tax-deferral. I've heard some supposed experts on radio offer negative responses to variable annuities because of the fees. They will argue the fact that the extra ½ percent you may pay in a variable costs you way too much money in the long run. While it's true, it may cost you some return in the long run, the tax benefits, I believe more than make up for the extra fee. In the graph below, notice the difference between the two options. This represents a $10,000 deposit for thirty years at 10%, accounting for an extra ½% management fee on the VA.

Variable Annuity	**Mutual Fund (MF)**	**MF After Taxes**
$152,203	$174,494	$76,123

What happens when you cash out the variable annuity? Wouldn't you then have to pay taxes on the earnings over the $10,000 you invested and ultimately end up with less than the mutual fund? I would respond with another question. What if I don't cash it out, rather, just take an interest income from the variable? At 5% income, I would draw a taxable $7,610.15 per year toward my retirement. When I take 5% from the mutual fund (assuming they paid no dividends that year) I wouldn't have income tax, but may still have a capital gains tax of 20%. My gross income from the mutual fund would be $3,806.15 per year. Not to mention, if I take my income in the form of a split annuity, there would be even less taxation (I wont take time to discuss split annuities here)

Notes:

_____

_____

_____

_____

Another feature of a variable annuity is that the insurance company offers a minimum guarantee in the event of death. There are different variations of this benefit. However, the most common is that every seven years, the annuity will mark the balance of your account. Let's say you had the $261,967 shown above. Should anything happen where the owner of the account were to die, the insurance company guarantees the beneficiary, that for the next seven years, they can't receive any less than the $261,967. If the market were to crash after this adjustment point by the company and the value of the account fell due to the market to $199,000. The beneficiaries would be assured not to receive less than the $261,967.

Equity Index Annuity (EIA):

This form of annuity is a new breed that first began coming into the market place around 1995 and 1996. They are quickly becoming one of the favorite annuity investments, especially amongst investors who tend to be more conservative. If you would be content with an average rate of return of 6 to 9 percent, and like the idea of no downside risk on your money, then the equity index may be for you.

In an EIA, your return is tied to a market index. I'll use the DOW as an example. It's important to note that each EIA in the marketplace has its own unique features and you should study the investment material before making a decision on which one may be best for you. A typical EIA would work like this:

Assume you invest $10,000. If the monthly average of the market goes up 5% you would earn 5%. If the monthly average goes up 10% you

Notes:

_____

_____

_____

_____

would earn 10% and so on. The key being, if the market goes down in the year of your investment, you would not lose one penny.

What's the catch? EIA's have a cap on how much you can earn. Most of the ones I have seen and used for my clients have a cap on earnings at the time of this writing of anywhere from 10% – 14% Let's look as these a little more in detail.

There are three things you want to be aware of when looking to invest into an EIA: the cap rate, the participation rate and fees.

Cap Rate: This is the maximum amount of earnings you can achieve in the plan in one year. If the cap rate is 12%, and the monthly average of the market goes up 12% that year, then you would earn 12% but never more in a given year. However, in exchange for this cap the company is guaranteeing that in a year in which the market goes down, you won't lose anything. In this event, your balance would be the same as it was at the beginning of the year.

Participation Rate: This determines if you get all of the markets movement or just a percentage of it. Many EIA's have a 100% participation rate. However, some carry a lesser percentage like 50% to 85%. To illustrate, assume the market was up 10% the past year and you had a participation rate of 75%. This means you receive 75% of the markets positive movement. In this case, that would mean 75% of 10% or 7.5%. Sometimes, you can find an unlimited Cap Rate, but in exchange a 70% participation rate.

Fees: This is a fee the company charges that comes right off the top of your return. Assume you had a cap of 12% with a 100% participation

Notes:

_____

_____

_____

_____

rate but a 2% fee. The market that year climbed up 12%. You are capped at 12%, but because of the fee, you would earn 10%.

I am not a believer in an EIA that has fees. Most of the ones I recommend to clients have no fees.

Finally, EIA's offer one other advantage. To help you understand the benefit, let me illustrate. Well assume you're in an EIA that has a CAP of 10% and a 100% participation rate with no fees, and you invest $10,000. Let's say the first year, the market goes up 10% from a DOW of 11,000 to 12,100. Your balance at the end of year 1 is now $11,000 ($10,000 invested plus 10% interest on $1,000).. The second year, the market falls 20% to 9680. You would still have a balance of $11,000. You see you capture your earnings each year. So, you not only keep your principle but the interest you've earned as well. Also, you begin earning on your money the next year from a DOW of 9680. You don't have to get back up to where you left the DOW at 12,100 to break even. You never lost money to begin with.

Now, the third year the DOW goes up 10% again to 10,650. You now earn another 10% on your money to raise you to a balance of $12,100.

This is one example of EIA's. There are many forms and combinations to choose from. EIA's cannot be purchased on your own; you must buy them through a financial advisor. I would highly recommend asking friends for someone you could trust who may offer these investments.

When searching for EIA's, I would strongly recommend not purchasing one with a surrender charge longer than 10 years. It all depends on your financial goals.

Notes:

_____

_____

_____

_____

I find one of the best features of annuities, for those who have had trouble saving, is the fact that your money is penalized for early withdrawal. An annuity is similar to an IRA in that if you withdraw before 59 ½ you would not only pay taxes due, but also a 10% penalty. This gives you a slap on the wrist if you try to spend the money. Please remember that annuities are for long-term investing. They can offer a great advantage and vehicle for part of your investment portfolio. However, I would never recommend them as the only vehicle. Again, here comes that word, BALANCE.

Notes:

_____

_____

_____

_____

CHAPTER NINE

RETIREMENT PLANS, THE GOOD AND THE BAD

Are you confused by the wide array of retirement plan terminology going around today? Do you fully understand 401-K's, IRA's, 403-B's, and Roth IRA's?

If you do, then why not be a financial planner or advisor? If you're like most people today, you too are confused by most of it. In this chapter, we will be spending our time looking more generally at the benefits of retirement plans, rather than the specifics of each. However, I will spend some time talking about the three most popular plans, the IRA, Roth IRA and 401-K.

First, allow me to share some terminology. Whenever I speak of "qualified money," I am talking about assets inside some form of retirement account like those I mentioned above. This would be money that you invested either before taxes were taken out of your paycheck, or after taxes were taken out, but then you received a deduction on your tax return. Therefore, in the eyes of the government, the money inside a qualified retirement plan has never been taxed. When we say non-qualified, we are speaking about your investments where taxes were taken out before you received your money to invest.

Notes:

_____

_____

_____

_____

IRA's and 401-K's are not investments.

It is very common for people to approach me at one of my seminars and ask me if I think an IRA is a good investment. I have to help them understand, that these qualified plans, are not an investments. Rather, they are designations attached to an investment.

If you went into a bank and asked them for an IRA, they would most likely sell you a CD (Certificate of Deposit). Then you would sign a piece of paper making that CD a qualified IRA. A stockbroker on the same investment might sell you a stock or mutual fund. You then sign a piece of paper making it an IRA. Just about any investment can be purchased as an IRA or qualified investment. So, to determine if an IRA is a good investment, I would first have to know "what" you have invested it in. The IRA is not the investment, the IRA is a shell wrapped around an already existing form of investment to make it a qualified investment.

Qualified money always grows tax-deferred. Tax-deferred means that while the money is in the account, it is not subject to taxes. If you had $10,000 in a qualified plan, and earned 8% interest that year, you would have earned $800. If the money were in a non-qualified account, you would, in most cases, be required to pay taxes on the $800 you earned. This would be true whether you used the money or left it invested. In a qualified account, the money is allowed to grow without taxes until you someday pull it out. This is called tax-deferred.

The advantages of tax deferral are tremendous. Say you invested $100 per month at 10% from age 25 to 65 in a taxable account. This would mean you would have to claim your interest earnings each year and pay 33% in taxes (counting federal and state taxes). The balance of your

Notes:

_____

_____

_____

_____

account when you're age 65 would be $241,375. You could then take an income of 6% per year or $14,482 per year toward your retirement without touching your principal.

However, say you invested the same $100 per month for the same period of time, receiving the same 10%, but did it in a tax-deferred plan. You would have $632,408. Assuming the same 6% interest income, that would provide an income in retirement of $37,945 per year, a difference of $23,463 per year! Which income would you prefer?

Tax-Deferred Vs. Taxable Returns

The Sooner You Start The Better!

For every ten-year period of time that you put off investing for your retirement, you will lose approximately 65% of your potential retirement income.

Look at the charts below. In both cases, the investor was placing $100 per month into some form of a retirement plan

25 year old at 65 = $632,408   **35 year old at 65 = $226,049**
30 year old at 65 = $379,664   **40 year old at 65 = $132,683**

In each case, the person who started 10 years later, ended up with approximately 35% of the amount generated by the person who started 10 years earlier. A 65% loss!

Many people don't get serious about investing for retirement until they reach their late 30's or early 40's. Some wait even longer. Why?

Notes:

_____

_____

_____

_____

Retirement is so far off they believe they have plenty of time. Or, it could be they have gotten themselves so deep in debt, they have no choice but to focus on today and worry about tomorrow later.

Always remember, balance is the key in everything! It doesn't matter which side of the horse you fall off of, it hurts and causes pain to do so. The key is to stay in the saddle. To do that, you must have balance.

If you spend too much time at work, trying to provide the best for your family, you may not have a family to provide for. Balance is the key!

You learned in earlier chapters the importance of beginning your investment program BEFORE you are out of debt. You balance your financial freedom money by putting half toward debt and half toward investments. Once your debts are paid off, continue to balance how you use the monthly cash flow that you have now freed up. Place half into investments and use the other half in ways that can provide a quality of life for your family today.

Sources of Retirement Income

There are three main sources of retirement income.

- **The Government**
- **Your Employer**
- **Your Individual Investments**

Notes:

_____

_____

_____

_____

Government Support

When we speak of the government, we are speaking of Social Security income.

If you ask most any American today if they are depending on Social Security for their retirement, the answer will be no! However, if you ask them what they are doing to provide for their retirement, the answer will be something insignificant.

Most of you reading this book are so busy trying to meet the financial demands of today that it's hard to look into the future and worry about tomorrow. People struggling to make ends meet in retirement are in that position, because by the time retirement was starring them in the face it was too late to do anything about it. Therefore, they end up depending on Social Security.

While I believe the chances of Social Security being there for the next 30 or 40 years are good, it is important we understand that if there was ever a financial drain on the United States, it wouldn't surprise me to see the Congress use some of the Social Security assets to bail out the country. As of the writing of this book, the economy has been shaky. However, Social Security seems to be in good shape for now.

The only true way to secure your retirement is by you taking care of business! You must get serious about your future and plan ahead. Whether Social Security is available in your future or not, it was never intended to provide your total financial needs in retirement. It was only intended to aid in it.

Notes:

_____

_____

_____

_____

Finally, new laws have been passed that are increasing the age at which time you can begin to draw your Social Security income.

Social Security Full Retirement and Reductions by Age
No matter what your full retirement age is, you may start receiving benefits as early as age 62

Year of Birth Note: Persons born on January 1 of any year should refer to the previous year.	Full Retirement Age	Age 62 Reduction Months	Monthly % Reduction	Total % Reduction
1937 or earlier	65	36	.555	20.00
1938	65 and 2 months	38	.548	20.83
1939	65 and 4 months	40	.541	21.67
1940	65 and 6 months	42	.535	22.50
1941	65 and 8 months	44	.530	23.33
1942	65 and 10 months	46	.525	24.17
1943-1954	66	48	.520	25.00
1955	66 and 2 months	50	.516	25.84
1956	66 and 4 months	52	.512	26.66
1957	66 and 6 months	54	.509	27.50

Notes:

_____

_____

_____

_____

1958	66 and 8 months	56	.505	28.33
1959	66 and 10 months	58	.502	29.17
1960 and later	67	60	.500	30.00

The biggest challenge for Social Security is not just the government trust fund to provide the income, but also the huge volume of Baby Boomers who have now begun retiring. This would mean fewer people in the work force supporting even more retirees. Then you must add the increasing life expectancy and period of time that an average retiree must be supported.

Your Employer and Individual Investments

The two most popular plans created for employees and offered by many employers, are the 401-K and the 403-B plans. Both plans are virtually identical. However, while any employer can offer 401-K plans, 403-B plans, are restricted to certain non-profit organizations such as education, religious and some medical institutions. For the purpose of this chapter, I will refer to either plan as the 401-K plan.

Money Down the Drain!

If I told you of an investment that would guarantee you a return of 25% per year, would you think that's a good deal? Would you make sure to find some money to invest in it? What if I guaranteed a 50% return each year? How would you feel about that? That is exactly what many people are being offered, and they are simply ignoring this FREE MONEY!

Notes:

_____

_____

_____

_____

It would always amaze me how many people I would counsel who had no idea if their employer even offered a 401-K plan. If they did believe one was offered, many had no idea if the employer was offering what is called a matching contribution. Worse yet, was when they did know that they could get this free money, but didn't participate in the plan. They were more focused on today than tomorrow, usually because of debt. They had allowed their financial life to become unbalanced.

If your employer contributes 50 cents on every dollar you invest, that could mean $600,000 in retirement instead of $400,000. A FREE $200,000! Is the new boat or car and the payments your making worth $200,000?

Finally, with an employer-sponsored plan, you have tax breaks in that the money invested into the 401-K is taken off the top of your reportable income. If you earned $40,000 and contributed $4,000 to your retirement plan, you would receive a W-2 showing you only made $36,000. The taxes on the other $4,000 are deferred. This offers even greater advantages that we will discover, along with IRA's next.

More FREE MONEY!
Uncle Sam Can Help You Pay For Your Retirement.

If you don't have a retirement plan available through your employer, it's no problem! The U.S. Government has a plan for you. It's called the traditional IRA or ROTH IRA. First, let's look at the traditional.
What would you say if I offered you a guaranteed return of 37% on your money, the year in which you invested it? That's exactly what a traditional IRA can offer.

Notes:

_____

_____

_____

_____

146

Assume you are in a 27% tax bracket, and are investing around $80 per month or $1,000 per year. If you were to turn your investment into a traditional IRA, you would receive a tax deduction. If you earned $40,000 in the year, you could deduct the $1,000 you invested and only have to pay taxes on $39,000. At 27% tax, you would have saved $270 in taxes. This $270 would have gone to the government as taxes. However, because you invested in the IRA, the government will allow you to keep the $270 in your IRA plan. This is money growing with interest for your retirement, that you would have otherwise never seen.

Further, you have received a guaranteed return in the first year of 37%. How? Had you not invested the $1,000 in an IRA, you would have received only $730 extra in your take-home paycheck. The $270 you now get to keep represents a 37% return on an investment of $730.

Preferential Tax Treatment

Tax Bracket	Contribution	Tax Savings	After-tax cost	Return from Tax Savings
27%	$1,000	$270	$730	36.99%

IRA's have limits on the amount you may contribute each year. As of this writing, they are $3,000 per year, per person. However, if you are over the age of 50 you are allowed $3,500 per year, per person. The government is willing to help you build your retirement, don't let your free money escape!

Notes:

_____

_____

_____

Chapter Ten

Planning For Your Loved Ones (The Value Of Proper Insurance)

For a period of a little over eight years, Connie and I went around the country working with couples and helping them learn how to build family businesses from their homes. It was a very rewarding time and helps you develop business skills that can provide extra cash flow for debt reduction or family needs.

One of the families we had the privilege of working with was from Southern California. They were a hard-working, middle class American family with four children. We grew very close to them and loved the family. The first tragedy occurred when we received a call stating their second son was killed while serving his country in the Marines. Just before I began the writing of this chapter, Connie and I received another very disturbing phone call from a common friend who informed us that the father, while still in his 40's, died of a heart attack.

Tragedies like this are hard to deal with and even more difficult to explain. Unfortunately, the father of this family died with virtually no life insurance. In this chapter, I would like to investigate the need for insurance, not only life insurance but other forms of coverage as well.

Notes:

_____

_____

_____

_____

How long could your family continue without you? If you are the primary breadwinner in the home and you were to die tomorrow, how capable is your spouse of replacing your income? Even if the surviving spouse did go back to work, would this mean they would be forced to sell the house and move? If your spouse is a stay at home spouse raising the children, please don't underestimate his or her value to the family! Just try living without them for one month and see how well you keep up on the family affairs! Each parent in the home is a valuable part of the infrastructure of the home and needs to be insured!

I find insurance can be one of the most misunderstood and improperly utilized financial vehicles. Many people either have an extreme amount of it or very little at all. The role of insurance is not necessarily to set some one up in the penthouse suite at our death, nor should it be to simply cover burial expenses. There is a plan and purpose that should go with each policy. We must identify the end result we desire in the event of a major loss and then prepare and implement a plan to carry out our wishes.

The House

When insuring your home and its possessions, check to see if your policy is based on actual cash value or replacement value. There's a big difference!

This past Christmas, we experienced our first, and I hope last, fire in our home. While entertaining four other couples one night, Connie and I at the same time, both stood up and shouted we smell something burning! We roamed through the house searching for the location of the smell. Our senses led us to the dinning room where to my amazement; the

Notes:

_____

_____

_____

_____

dinning room table had a big ball of fire dancing on the top of it. I quickly sprang into action to handle the matter, saving our house, family and all of our guests from certain devastation (well maybe it didn't quite happen that way). The next day, Connie called our insurance company. Since the table was not destroyed and could be refinished, we eventually received a check for $1,000 for repairs.

Had the table been destroyed, one of two things could have happened; if our policy read actual cash value, we may have received less than what the table cost us. The original cost of the table was $2,500. If insured for actual cash value, the insurance company would have factored in how old the table was and instead of replacing the table, the company would have given us an amount based on what the table would have been worth as a used table.

While I'm not sure of the exact numbers, a $2,500 table that is now five years old may only be worth $1,400 in the eyes of the insurance company. If the table were 10 years old, we may have only gotten $750.

By contrast, let's say we had replacement value in our policy. We paid $2,500 for the table, but the same table five years later, now cost us $3,000. We would receive a check to replace the table with one of like kind and quality, without concern over the current cost. While it cost a bit more to carry the replacement value coverage, most people would agree that the cost of homeowners or renters insurance is nominal to the potential value and therefore I would strongly recommend the replacement value be in your policy.

Notes:

_____

_____

_____

_____

Auto or Vehicle Insurance

While homeowners and renters insurance may be inexpensive, auto insurance is just the opposite. There's a reason for that. Houses don't move and aren't controlled or driven by motorists on cell phones, eating fast food or applying their makeup while driving. Also, there are far fewer residences in America than cars! Learning how to tame the monstrous cost of auto insurance is critical to sound financial management.

The deductible you carry on your insurance is one of the key ingredients to keeping costs down. I can't tell you the number of times I have had individuals or couples in my office who aren't, in my opinion, utilizing their deductibles properly.

Most people carry a $100 or maybe a $250 deductible on their cars. When I ask them how many accidents they have had in the past five years, it's not unusual for them to say none! Why then carry such a low deductible? By raising the deductible from $100 to $500, they could see premium savings of anywhere form $300 to $600 per year. That's as much as $50 per month that could be going into the asset column and in 10 to 18 months, you would have saved the entire cost of the deductible and have it working for you. Obviously, if you tend to be accident prone, you may want to keep the lower deductible. There is little reason for any reasonably safe driver to pay the higher premiums for lower deductibles.

Another way to reduce premiums is to determine if you need Broad Form or Basic Collision. If I had to guess, I would say 80% or greater of the people I counsel, have Broad Form Collision. Broad Form means that if

Notes:

_____

_____

_____

_____

you are in an accident, that is not your fault, you are not required to pay your deductible. You are only required to meet your deductible if you were the driver that caused the accident.

Basic coverage on the other hand means that you would have to pay the deductible regardless of who was at fault. Basic Collision will lower your premiums and makes sense for reasonably safe drivers. If you can't bring yourself to raise your deductible limits, at least consider Basic Collision. If the other driver is at fault, you have the right to ask them to cover your deductible and make you whole.

Uninsured Motorists

Not every state has laws concerning uninsured motorists coverage. If your state does, this is insurance that is for YOU! Not the uninsured guy. It is very inexpensive and yet the typical policy will only have 20/40 coverage. This means, if an uninsured motorist was to hit your car and you were to need hospitalization, you would only receive from your company a maximum of $20,000 in protection per person or $40,000 if more than one person was involved. If you have 20/40 uninsured motorists, your premium is probably only around $15 - $20 per year. To raise it up to $100,000/$300,000 wont cost you more than about double that same amount. Remember, it's protection for your family. At these low rates, it may be something to consider.

Liability Coverage

It was a cold day during the first week of February. Connie and I had Kelly and Kris in the back seat and were making the drive from our home in Ft. Wayne, Indiana to the Detroit area. I was working for a

Notes:

_____

_____

_____

_____

financial services firm at the time and they had requested the relocation. The move was fine with us, as our entire extended family lived in southeastern Michigan.

The trip that day was to spend the weekend with a realtor to look at homes. Since that's where Grandmas and Grandpas lived, it would be certain suicide not to bring their grandchildren with us.

Our accident occurred in the small town of Waterville, Ohio, just outside Toledo. We were on a two lane highway and up ahead approximately ¾ of a mile, I could see a light that had just turned red. As we approached the light, there was a car that had already arrived at the light and had come to a complete stop. The closer I got to the light the more I slowed down until I was simply creeping up to the light at less than 10 miles per hour.

Suddenly, just as I was about to come to a stop, I noticed a patch of sheer ice from me to the car in front of me. I hit the brakes and began to slide. Then I began pumping the brakes (anti-locks weren't on this car) and unfortunately, "bumped" the car in front. The impact was so slight; it was about as hard as you would bump another car if you approached to give them a push.

I got out of the car and neither bumper had been damaged, nor had any of the residue snow on either bumper even fallen off. I waved into the back window of the other car and shouted "sorry" and went back to my car. Both of my children were sleeping in the back and neither one woke up.

When the light turned green, the car in front didn't move. Suddenly, a female riding in the passenger seat got out and came back to Connie's

Notes:

_____

_____

_____

_____

side of the car and told us her husband had hurt his back! I jumped out and ran to her car and opened the driver's door to find a male slumped over the armrest to his right and moaning. The moans were about the furthest thing from reality I had ever heard. His wife approached me and said we need to call an ambulance! "Uh-Oh," I said, I just bumped into the wrong guy.

Shortly, a police officer arrived and took over the scene. He asked me to join him in his squad car after the ambulance arrived. He said he had to write me a ticket, however, he clearly wrote, "Impact 0 to 5 MPH". He had been sitting up on top of the hill of the street crossing ours watching for someone to run a yellow or red light and had seen the whole thing. "Mr. Whipple," he said, "you unfortunately just hit the wrong guy." I received no fine or even points for the accident.

About six weeks later, we received a letter from a law firm in Toledo. We were being sued for $1,000,000.00! Not only was the husband claiming back injuries, but also, the wife was claiming whiplash! Connie began to cry believing we were about to lose our house and all our possessions. The end result was, after depositions and trips to Toledo to defend us, the suit was thrown out of court before it ever went to trial. We were blessed!

But Curt, you say, you had insurance! The insurance company would have paid for the accident and liability. True, but upon investigation, my liability coverage was $100,000/$300,000. This means it would only cover $100,000 per person or a total of $300,000 per accident. Do the math! If they won a $1,000,000 judgment and I only had $200,000 coverage for the two people involved, I'm left to cover the balance of

Notes:

_____

_____

_____

_____

$800,000! I would have spent the rest of my life paying for this couples future!

The Value of Umbrella Liability Coverage

I highly recommend each and every person carry an umbrella policy in conjunction with their auto insurance. You can buy this coverage usually in million dollar increments. In a moment, I'll tell you just how inexpensive it is! However, first, it's important to know that even though the coverage is purchased from your auto insurance company, the protection follows you no matter where or how you may be sued.

If you get mad and call your neighbor a name, if someone gets food poisoning while eating at you home, a slip and fall occurs on your property, it doesn't matter! Your umbrella policy follows you and protects you in the event someone brings suits against you. It doesn't matter the reason.

Are you ready? Depending on the insurance company your with, the cost is about $100 - $200 per year for an individual, or $150 – $250 per year for a couple! Talk about cheap peace of mind! We live in a very litigious society. People don't need much of a reason to bring suit against you. Many people are looking for the easy way to retirement. Don't let your future be taken by them.

Life Insurance

The cost of life insurance has been dropping. This is, in large part, due to longer life expectancies as a result of modern medicine. In 1994, there were 357 million people in the world over the age of 65. In 2000, there

Notes:

_____

_____

_____

_____

were 418 million people in the world over the age of 65. The world's population of people 65 and older is increasing by over 1,000 persons every hour! Under mortality conditions of the year 1900, 41% of newborns would reach age 65 compared to 80% under the mortality conditions of 1991.

The insurance industry puts out their life expectancy tables every 20 years. The last one was published in 2000. A newborn girl born in the year 2000, according to the insurance industry, has a life expectancy of 113! Because of these longer life spans, the cost of life insurance continues to decrease. There are two major forms of life insurance. They are Term and Whole Life.

Term Life Insurance

For most of you reading this book, the first insurance policy you should own would be Term Life. The younger you are, the more apt Term Life would be appropriate for you. When we are younger, we tend to be "getting started" and trying to make ends meet. Money can tend to be tight while we strive to develop our career or mission in life.

Term insurance is very inexpensive while we are younger and climbs in cost, as we get older. It is also purchased for a specific "term" of time. So eventually, we will lose it. Term insurance was designed and offered to cover an individual for a period of time when they didn't have the assets to protect their family in the event of a premature death.

Notes:

_____

_____

_____

_____

As of the writing of this book, some typical annual premiums for a 15-year term policy were:

$250,000 of coverage
(Male)

AGE	COST
30	$ 162.50
40	$ 225.00
50	$ 505.00
60	$1,122.50

As you can see, the older one gets, the cost goes up. However, it is important to note that the above rates are guaranteed for the "term" of 15 years.

In my opinion there is no excuse, at these rates, for anyone to leave their family unprotected in the event of their death. In earlier chapters, I showed you how to "find" money you didn't realize you had. Use some of that money and make sure you protect the ones you love, TODAY!

If you bought term insurance before the year 2000, it is a good idea to get some competitive quotes. Since the new mortality tables came out in 2000, showing longer life expectancies, premiums offered have dropped in price. You can possibly save additional money for the asset column, or, have additional money to buy the added protection you may need.

While term insurance is temporary, the industry offers three types of permanent insurance. They are Whole Life, Universal Life and Variable Life. Let's briefly look at each one:

Notes:

_____

_____

_____

_____

Whole Life

While many financial professionals will beat up on the evils of Whole Life, I believe there can be a time and a place for it. However, first lets look at how it works. Then the reasons " to buy or not to buy."

Whole life insurance has a fixed cost for a death benefit. Once you purchase the policy, the cost of the insurance can never go up. Your premiums can never change because of the fixed cost. This means, if purchased at a younger age, you hold the lower premiums no matter how old you get.

Whole Life policies also build what is called "cash value." A fixed amount of every premium you pay, goes toward the insurance itself. The balance then goes into the cash value column of the policy and earns interest. The rate of return on cash value is usually a bit better than you can get in a bank CD (Certificate of Deposit) and grows tax-free until it equals the total amount you have put into the policy. Everything that exceeds the premium you've paid would grow tax-deferred and would be taxable upon withdrawal, unless you took the money out through policy loans.

Loans are a tax-free form of withdrawal. At some point the cash value usually grows large enough, if you wanted to, you could stop paying your premiums and the interest earnings on the cash value would pay the premiums for you. If you continue to pay into the policy and develop a large cash value balance, you could then also use the policy to provide you a retirement income on a tax-free basis. You could do this while maintaining the policy, which would then pay out a death benefit when you die.

Notes:

_____

_____

_____

_____

Here's how a Whole Life policy might look on a chart paid annually.

Age	*Premium*	*Cost/Expenses*	*Amount to Cash Value*
30	$600.00	$375.00	$225.00
31	$600.00	$375.00	$225.00
32	$600.00	$375.00	$225.00
33	$600.00	$375.00	$225.00

Some "professionals" claim that Whole Life Insurance is a waste of money or a bad deal for most consumers. I don't believe Whole Life Insurance is the culprit, I believe the people who sell it to consumers inappropriately is where the problem lies. Every form of insurance has its place, and need in society. The key is applying the right insurance to each individual situation properly.

In my opinion the absolute greatest, although not only, value for Whole Life Insurance is in the area of estate planning. By following the ideas and plans presented in this book, you will someday be financially free. Although it may be hard to imagine, you could someday build a net worth of over $1,000,000.00.

Let's assume you accomplish that. Assume you retired and eventually at your death, you died with a net worth of $3,000,000.00 (nice thought eh?). What would you say, if I said your children would have to give $1,000,000.00 of your net worth back to the government at your death? Now your children get only $2,000,000.00. Not fair? Maybe, but it's what can happen if you die with a sizable estate. Now, what if I told you that for $200,000.00 you could provide your children with $1.2 million to pay both the tax and the original cost of the $200,000.00, so they now

Notes:

_____

_____

_____

_____

get to keep the whole 3 million? That's exactly what Whole Life Insurance can do. If you find your estate does not end up as large as you expected, you can cancel the policy and receive the cash value it has built up. You can then invest the cash value as you see fit.

Whole Life is also a good foundation to provide the expenses surrounding your death in older ages. Assume the average funeral cost about $6,000 to $10,000. If you bought a Whole Life policy for $25,000 to $50,000, it would at least guarantee to cover the cost of your funeral in future years. If in older ages when term becomes too expensive for you to maintain, you would still have the Whole Life to fall back on.

The drawback to Whole Life is that it is considered to be expensive coverage. Especially when you are raising a young family and trying to find a way to make ends meet. Therefore, it makes it almost impossible for the average person to cover all of their insurance needs with Whole Life. Should your family need $250,000 of coverage to meet their needs should you die, the premiums on Whole Life may make it impossible to afford.

Universal Life

Universal Life works very similar to Whole Life. The major difference is that the cost of insurance is based on your age. Each year that you own the policy the cost goes up based on you being one year older. When you first purchase a Universal Life policy, the cost of the insurance inside the plan would always be cheaper than the cost of the Whole Life insurance. This would leave more money in the early years going into the cash value account to earn interest. However, as you get

Notes:

_____

_____

_____

_____

older each year, the cost of the insurance increases. This means less money going into cash value.

The idea in this insurance is that if you buy it when you're younger and have a much higher amount going into cash value, it accelerates the growth of your cash value and provides more money to help cover the cost of increasing insurance in older ages.

This is how a Universal Life policy might look.

Age	Premium	Cost/Expenses	Amount to Cash Value
30	$600.00	$125.00	$475.00
31	$600.00	$130.00	$470.00
32	$600.00	$137.00	$463.00
33	$600.00	$146.00	$454.00

Eventually, the cost of insurance will exceed the amount of the premium being paid.

Age	Premium	Cost/Expenses	Amount to Cash Value
59	$600.00	$627.00	<$27.00>

The idea is that the cash value in your account, by this time, would be large enough that the insurance company can take the premium shortage from your cash value. In this case, the amount would be $27. Each year however, the amount taken increases. However, the cash value would be large enough (i.e.$50,000) to cover the additional cost and still grow with interest. Universal Life insurance is permanent insurance and will last the rest of your life, provided that the cash value never drops to zero. Should the cash value hit zero, you would have to make the higher

Notes:

_____

_____

_____

_____

premium payments to keep the policy in force. Otherwise the policy would "lapse" or fall apart and be canceled. However, the policy is designed that as long as you make your premium payments, it should never be in danger of lapsing.

The interest rate paid on the cash value of a Universal Life is similar to Whole Life. Again, the rate of return is usually a bit better than you get in a bank CD (Certificate of Deposit) and grows tax-free until it equals the total amount you have put into the policy. Everything that exceeds the premium you've paid would be taxable upon withdrawal, unless you took the money out through policy loans or as a result of death. Loans are a tax-free form of withdrawal. At some point, the cash value usually grows large enough and if you wanted, you could stop paying premiums and the interest earnings on the cash value would pay the premiums for you. If you develop a large cash value balance, then you could also use the policy to provide you a retirement income on a tax-free basis. You could do this, while maintaining the policy, which would then pay out a death benefit when you die, just like the Whole Life policy.

Universal Life policies, in my opinion, are not as valuable as Whole Life when it comes to estate planning. The reason is because of the increasing cost of insurance within the policy. People who are older and have a sizable net worth usually purchase insurance in order to cover estate taxes. They need ways to protect their assets from taxation. As you recall, the cost of insurance in a Universal Life policy climbs each year. The older you get, the faster the premiums increase. When done for estate planning, the insured plans only contribute to the policy for a stated number of years and then let the policy pay for itself. Because the cost of the Whole Life policy never goes up, the insured can be more confident the insurance they need, will be there when needed.

Notes:

_____

_____

_____

_____

Variable Life

The final form of life insurance we will look at is Variable Life. Quite simply, Variable Life and Universal Life are the exact same form of insurance. Each policy works the same in the cost of insurance and how much the insurance may cost within the policy. The major difference is that the cash value in a Variable Life policy is invested in a form of mutual fund rather than at a fixed interest rate.

For many policyholders, the Variable Life became the policy of choice in the late '80's and '90's. This represented what I believe was the greatest "Bull" market run in U.S. history. Instead of earning 6% to 7% interest on their cash value, policyholders felt they could earn 12% to 15% by investing their cash value in the stock or bond market.

Each policyholder could pick the mutual funds to place their cash value in and therefore, the degree of risk on their cash value. The higher the risk of the account they chose, the faster the potential rise in value of the account. However, in negative years in the market, they could also lose value in the cash value account.

You could be heavily invested in technology or overseas stocks if you liked. Sure enough, those who placed their cash value in the market from 1981 through 1999 most likely reaped handsome rewards in the growth of their cash value. However, policyholders were yanked back to reality, when the stock market took a dive in March 2000 through 2002. Values in mutual funds fell by as much as 20% - 40%, or more. This meant the planned cash values of these policies were, in some cases, devastated.

Notes:

_____

_____

_____

_____

If you remember from Universal Life, if the cash value of the policy ever goes to zero, you can lose your insurance. If you were 45 in 1985, and bought a Variable Life policy, and now in 2002, you were 62 and lost significant amounts of cash value (the thing you need to help cover the cost of insurance as it goes up each year), you could be facing the need to draw tax-free income from your policy. That need is now greatly hindered if not destroyed, and you may now have to contribute to the policy for the rest of your life to maintain it, as the cost of insurance continues to go up with each birthday you celebrate.

Just this past Sunday, I had someone stop me in the isle at church and mentioned their insurance policy (purchased from someone else) just lapsed. They had a variable life policy and as a result of the market losses in 2000, the cash value dropped to a level that could not support the policy. Over 5 years of premiums just went up in smoke.

Please don't take these last paragraphs as meaning I would avoid or disagree with Variable Life policies. The younger you are, the more valuable this type of insurance may be. I personally don't believe in using Variable Life in older ages. The risk is too great.

Remember, every form of insurance has its place. I only hope to call your attention to some of the risks associated with Variable Life. Make sure you consult an insurance professional to get the information you need to determine which form of insurance is right for you. Variable Life can be the right policy when used in the right circumstance.

Notes:

_____

_____

_____

_____

How Much Is Enough?

I have heard every imaginable idea on how to determine how much life insurance you need. Everything from I'm too young to worry to you need at least six times your annual income. Frankly, none of the so-called "general ideas" are appropriate. Each individual situation requires different calculations and needs.

I don't think it would be possible to discuss in this chapter all the different combinations that may be needed to identify every possible situation. However, I'll give it the ole college try.

First, I feel a trusted insurance advisor can be invaluable, and I would strongly recommend professional help in determining your needs and finding the right plan for you and your family. The financial devastation can be incomprehensible to your surviving family, not to mention the grief of loss. You want to make sure you are properly covered. One of the greatest concerns over choosing a life insurance professional is that many of us see the life agent on the same playing field as someone who sells used cars (maybe worse). However, I assure you there are far more honest and quality professionals in the life insurance market place than bad ones. We only seem to hear of the ones who took the public for a ride. The best advice I can give is to ask your closest friends and family who they use and can stand behind. This at least gives you a good starting point.

Should you decide to go it alone, and figure out your own needs, the Internet provides tremendous aids at your fingertips. Simply go into your search engine and type "Life Insurance Calculator" and you will have dozens of websites to choose from. Each offering a questionnaire

Notes:

_____

_____

_____

_____

to follow, and then it provides a final result of the amount (and sometimes type) of life insurance you need. Keep in mind that if you are single, your needs could be covered by any assets you may have. If you have very few assets, then an insurance policy is a good idea. I don't believe anyone would want to leave the burden of the final expenses to other family members. If you are married and or have a family that depends on you, it is critical you carry the proper amount of insurance.

Once you determine the amount of coverage needed. Then what form of insurance should you buy? Again, consulting a professional advisor is recommended. However, allow me to share some thoughts.

If you are a younger person and single and keeping the cost low is critical, then I recommend term insurance. It is far more important that you provide the proper amount of coverage than it is what form of coverage you have.

The perfect scenario in my mind would be to have a small amount of Whole Life or Universal Life insurance. A small amount would be enough insurance to cover $15,000 to $25,000 of immediate expenses. After 15 to 18 years, the policy may have enough cash-value that you could stop paying premiums and the cash value earnings would pay the premiums for the rest of your life. Now, you have covered the final expenses. The premiums you were paying are now freed up to invest toward retirement or reduce your retirement overhead.

The balance of your insurance needs should then be covered with term insurance. The combination of the two policies would provide the necessary coverage a very reasonable cost.

Notes:

_____

_____

_____

_____

The older one gets, the less I believe variable life should be a part of their insurance portfolio. The risk associated with variable life can be too great. To me, mixing one of the most conservative products with a higher risk product just doesn't seem to make sense.

Allow me to share one final word on this subject. I have seen some real tragedies in the use of variable life by insurance agents. They have been representing this form of insurance to all ages as a form of investment. While insurance can be considered an investment in protecting and providing for our loved ones, it should NOT be considered in the same form of investing as stocks, mutual funds or annuities. When an insurance agent sells a younger person $500,000 of variable life insurance with premiums of two, three, even four thousand dollars, it can represent only one thing. A greedy agent who is more concerned with a commission than they are with their clients best interest in mind. The proper approach would be to provide the required coverage, in proper form, with the smallest amount of premium. This then can free up as many dollars as possible to go into investments in the asset column.

Questions to ask:

- How long would my spouse need to keep our current income? (Before he/she could generate an income)

- How would the income they earn compare to the needs of the family? What would be the shortfall?

- Do I feel it's important to payoff our mortgage?

- Do I have any outstanding loans I would like to payoff?

Notes:

_____

_____

_____

_____

- What would be the final expenses?

- Do I have investments that can be depended upon?

- If I'm married, and my spouse has to use our investments. Where does that leave him/her in retirement if used?

- Who will pay for my children's college? Would I like to leave a guarantee for them to be able to attend college as part of a legacy?

I strongly recommend the aid of a "trusted" insurance professional and estate-planning attorney for Wills or Trusts.

A Word About Credentials

Many insurance professionals can carry credentials after their name. Credentials like CLU, Chartered Life Underwriter or CFP, Certified Financial Planner (and the list goes on). While I do believe in these credentials and the extra knowledge it can provide to a professional, it says nothing about their integrity or concern for you. When looking for a professional, I would see these certifications as a bonus, not a necessity.

Disability Insurance

Ever met someone disabled? According to the National Organization on Disability (NOD), 50,000,000 Americans are currently disabled in some form. Do the math and you'll see that means one out of every five adults in America!

Notes:

_____

_____

_____

_____

The odds of you becoming disabled are far greater than you dying. Most of us have some form of death insurance. How many of us have disability insurance?

A disability can actually be more traumatic and costly than death. I've heard some people say that a disability can be a living death. If you were to die, it would cause your family a tremendous loss and as most people say, you never really get over it. If you leave proper life insurance, however, your family can move on financially.

If you're disabled, household costs don't go down (as in death: one less person to feed, one less car to buy and maintain, fewer clothes etc.), they go up. You're still here! How will you provide for your family if you are unable to work? If you're single, who will take care of you and at what expense.

Disability insurance is in my opinion "the" most overlooked form of protection in America. If purchased at younger ages, disability insurance can be reasonably priced, so it is recommended you investigate the cost and benefits early.

When looking for disability insurance, I highly recommend you consult a disability insurance expert. Their help is almost a necessity in making sure you get the right form of coverage, as it can be one of the hardest forms of protection to understand.

To begin educating yourself, I again recommend books at the library or on the Internet. It will give you a head start, so that when you do meet

Notes:

_____

_____

_____

_____

with a disability insurance professional you can have some understanding of the terms and issues.

Any enterprise (home) is built by wise planning, becomes strong through common sense, and profits wonderfully by keeping abreast of the facts. Proverbs 24:3&4 (The Living Bible)

Notes:

_____

_____

_____

_____

CHAPTER ELEVEN

MAKING COLLEGE POSSIBLE

At the writing of this book, my daughter, Kelly is 21 years old and my son, Kris, is 17. What I am about to share with you is based, to some extent, on personal experience and also fact. I'm in the middle of the college run, and if you are a parent of college-age children, or are about to be, I can feel your pain.

The Value

I don't think too many adults today would argue over the value of a college education. More than just training for a career direction, it can help us develop skills and disciplines that we can use throughout critical areas of our life.

Approach any major company today and the first item it looks for on a resume is the college degree. However, with rare exception, do I find which college the degree comes from to be critical.

For the first part of this chapter, please allow me some leeway in the discussion of college. Don't think, with what I'm about to say, that I don't believe in the value or the importance of a college degree. However, I do believe many children are being pushed into a direction "they" would not have chosen, and many parents are getting a "guilt trip" if they don't pay the way for their children, or force them into college.

Notes:

_____

_____

_____

_____

Allow me to address this issue first. Then we will come back and talk about how to make college possible financially.

Why College?

I graduated from Biola University in La Mirada, California. My training was in the field of radio and television broadcasting. Where am I today? I'm in the field of financial planning! Except for my first seven years out of college, I am self-employed and working in a field that doesn't even require a college degree.

You probably remember my mention of Robert Kiyosaki. Author of "Rich Dad, Poor Dad." Kiyosaki also has a degree. However, he built his wealth in the area of real estate. Again, no degree required.

Why do so many parents insist on sending their children to college? We already discussed one reason, which is increased potential for wider employment. Most individuals will not end up self-employed as Kiyosaki and I have. However, some parents will force their children to attend a college they don't desire, and pursue a field they have very little interest in. Why? At the heart of every parent is the desire to spare our children the mistakes we have made in our lifetimes. We don't want them to hurt or travel a rough road. We want them to find the easy path to their future. Therefore, we can sometimes put pressure on our "children" (yes, they are still children at this point who need our love and direction). Most children aren't sure of the direction they want to take at age 18, so we as parents feel a duty to help them go the way <u>we think</u> they should.

I believe mistakes are a part of life, and we would be harming our children if we smothered them to such a degree as to not allow them the

Notes:

_____

_____

_____

_____

room to make their own mistakes! Imagine a baby who is learning to walk, and we decide we don't want her to fall and hurt herself. So, each time she shows a sign of trying to walk, we run over and grab her and deliver her to where she needs to go. We'd have a society of 30-40-and 50-year olds crawling their way around town, always looking for someone to come and carry them through life.

Sometimes, we stress the importance of college because we want our children to have it better in life than we did. We want them to make more money. This then would allow them to buy more "stuff." Then they could have more stress than we did, as a result of managing all the extra stuff.

The final reason we, as parents, can sometimes feel the pressure to send our kids to college is because all our friends are sending their kids, and what kind of parents would we be if we didn't do the same? Here's a question. Do you want your children to learn they should be doing everything their friends are doing? That can sometimes be scary!

Parents, It's Time To Stop the Guilt Trip And Take The Pressure Off Our Children.

Yes! A college education can be very important. However, let's start talking about what's the best thing for "MY" child. Then, if college is in the future, we'll talk about "making it possible," financially.

Notes:

_____

_____

_____

_____

Your Child's Gifts

Each and every child born into this world is born with special gifts and talents. Some have a mind for numbers. Some have a mind for music or the arts. The field of gifts can range over a wide spectrum. As a parent, I feel my number one responsibility to my kids, is to help them identify where their gifts lie. By doing so, I can then help them identify what direction may be best for them, regardless of how much money they can make doing it. I would hope every parent's desire is for their children to find their gifts and find an occupation that allows them to use their gifts, and therefore find happiness in what they do.

The Key Is Not In How Much Money They Can Make!

I feel the greatest mistake kids can make is to target a field of work solely for the purpose of how much money they can make. I have never yet met anyone who is happy in life making tons of money but hates his or her job or career.

For sometime in my life, I worked in the area of selling employee benefits. Things like health, life, dental, disability and 401-K plans, I continued to do financial planning as well. The combined effort provided a very nice income. Yet, something was missing. I couldn't figure out what it was.

One thing I noticed was that I was becoming more "grouchy." I would put on my happy face and pull up the façade (false front) to let everyone believe I was happy and doing just great. However, inside I was miserable. I was (and still am) married to the most wonderful woman in the world, and yet my marriage was suffering deeply.

Notes:

_____

_____

_____

_____

I would get in shouting matches on the phone with people while at work. I would be short and sometimes mean to my assistant, Kathleen. It got so bad at times, that while in church on Sunday, I would watch a soloist singing and say, "Look at her smiling and singing. She's not really happy; she's probably just as miserable as I am."

WHY was I this way? I had a beautiful wife who loved me more than I knew. I had gorgeous children who would make any parent proud. I had a 3,300-square-foot home in a highly regarded location. I drove expensive cars. We took great and expensive family trips. Why then, was I so miserable?

I now know I was miserable because of two reasons. One, was my spiritual life was extremely weak. My relationship with my creator hung on a thin thread. I was trying to do everything in my own strength, and for the wrong reasons. In my own strength, I was mucking it all up!

Secondly, I was not using my gifts and not working in an area that brought joy and contentment (usually associated with using your gifts). Instead, I was working in an area that made good money. Why? I was more interested in working at something that "I believed" would bring me the greatest paycheck! I felt the key to my happiness was more money! I thought that's what would make Connie happy. What a joke! She is happiest when I am happy and content. This way, she gets the man she married.

In 2000, I felt led to begin writing this book (yes, it took me three years to complete). Deep down inside, I think I knew I needed to give something back to society rather than always looking for ways to take.

Notes:

_____

_____

_____

_____

More and more, I was running into people who were in financial bondage and going deeper and deeper into debt each year. I read many articles and books on the subject of debt. Recalling my own past, in my '20's and early '30's, I felt people who never personally experienced debt or financial bondage must have written many of these books. I didn't agree with many of the ideas or methods presented by the so-called "experts" in the subject.

It All Changed In 2000

The year 2000 marked a turning point in my life. Healthcare rates were, and probably still are, skyrocketing each and every year. Employers were finding it more and more difficult to pay the premiums necessary. I recognized that national healthcare could be coming down the pipe and felt my income would be in jeopardy. Back in the late '80's when financial planning was my main area of income, I had slowly shifted more of my time toward employee benefits. I felt employee benefits would offer me a more stable income and the ability to build more of it. I was very good at selling employee benefits. However, I wasn't the best, and it wasn't involving my gifts.

It was about that time, the summer of 2000, I was approached by two of my financial planning clients to have a part in a charitable convention. They asked me if I would conduct a workshop at the convention on personal finances and financial planning. I was to teach two classes, each about one hour in length. Being it was for a good cause, I felt compelled to accept the offer to help.

I began to put together what I felt would be the subject matter of each class. Things like stocks, bonds and mutual funds. Teaching the

Notes:

_____

_____

_____

_____

difference between A, B and C shares (we spoke on these in Chapter 7). While this can be educational and necessary, it doesn't provide for the most exciting seminar.

As I was preparing, it hit me. I don't want to teach this "stuff." If we're going to teach, lets teach things that will truly help those who attend. So, I threw out all of the notes and fancy handouts I had prepared and simply handwrote two pages of ideas and principles I believed would truly help those in attendance. I called the workshop "You'll Never Have Financial Freedom By Paying Off Your Debt." Catchy, eh?

At the end of the first class, each and every person there was so excited about what they had learned; they asked me what I would be teaching in the next hour. Not one of them left the room! The next group showed up and joined the first. I then taught the second class on a different subject. At the end of the second class, there was so much excitement about the money lessons, that those from the first class relayed what they had learned and I was asked to teach the first class a second time for those who missed it. Many of the participants from the first class stayed and went through it a second time.

I absolutely take no credit for the value or excitement in the three classes. It was truly a blessing of God. I just happened to be the fortunate one doing the teaching.

Notes:

_____

_____

_____

_____

What's all this got to do with college?
Stick with me; I'm almost there!

In February of 2001, I received a mailer from a company promoting the advantages of doing educational seminars. I was intrigued and looked into it further. While I felt my gift of teaching would be well utilized in this area, the big holdup was the cost. To design mailers, pay for them and provide a meal (recommended by the firm promoting the idea), costs would run about $8,000.00, and I would have no guarantee as to results.

Connie and I both have always had a special place in our hearts for senior citizens. Therefore, I decided to hold a seminar on how to invest safely for retirees (this turned out to be a great subject based on what happened in the stock market during the early years of our new century). The seminar was such a huge success, and I had so much fun doing it, that I now do them full-time and have hired another person to run the employee benefits side of our business.

I can't tell you the joy and happiness I now have. I'm spending my life "teaching" others. I teach the retired market how to invest safely; I teach people in debt how to be financially free and build their net worth, and I'm also honored to teach many classes in our church. It's what I was designed and made for, and I couldn't be happier.

My degree is in radio and television broadcasting!
Get the point?

I believe it is every parent's responsibility to help their child find where their gifts lie and then encourage them in a direction that will allow them to use those gifts, regardless of how much money they can make using

Notes:

_____

_____

_____

_____

them. That's when our kids will be the happiest. Isn't that what we desire most for our kids? Besides, this book is designed to teach that anyone, regardless of income, can be financially free!

College it is!

So, after all of that, what do we do if we determine that college is the right direction for our children? Here are some keys to follow.

Start Early
Begin to save as early as possible. It doesn't require as much savings as you think. In the chart below, I've shown what saving $100 per month can do based on starting at birth or waiting for 5, 10, and 15 years.

Age	Monthly Inv.	Value @ 18
0	$100	$48,008
5	$100	$27,292
10	$100	$13,387
15	$100	$ 4,054

Based on 8% annual return

As you can see, the difference between starting at the birth of any child creates an extra $21,000 over waiting just 5 years to begin.

Where to get help

Many parents make the mistake of thinking that the time to talk to the high school guidance counselor is when your child is in high school. Most parents even wait until the child 11th or 12th grade year. Major mistake.

Notes:

_____

_____

_____

_____

Wherever you live, I'm sure you pay property taxes on your home. If you rent, your landlord does and you can bet the taxes are rolled into your monthly rent checks. As a tax-paying resident, you have every right to go and see the high school guidance counselor at any time and while your child is at any age (even a newborn). Most guidance counselors take their job very seriously, and what they love most is helping parents and students find the right college and plan ahead to make it possible. Visit your guidance counselor early, and he or she will help you keep up on the facts and current trends in funding a college education.

Avoid common mistakes

Don't eliminate a school because the price is too high! Understand, that every college and university in the world is a business. As such, they are always looking for bright students who will reflect what they want their university to reflect. As such, they will compete to get your student. The best strategy you can take is to help your student become more marketable. The goal is to get as many different schools inviting your child to attend. Now the bidding begins. "Just how bad would you like my child?"

You may be saying, "That's great, Curt, but what if my son or daughter doesn't happen to have the best grades?" While grades can be important, they certainly aren't the only criteria. You can make your child more attractive to the college in several ways.

Groups and associations are highly regarded by colleges. Organizations like the Boy Scouts and Girl Scouts, church youth groups, 4H clubs and other social and civic groups. Any community or civic-minded group

Notes:

_____

_____

_____

_____

will all help. Schools want to know, was this student involved in the community and contribute, or did he sit home and play videogames all day?

Leadership positions are also highly regarded. Was the student involved in student council? Did she volunteer for community events or organizations such as the hospital, library, Rotary or Lions clubs?

Always fill out financial aid forms.

Never assume that your student can't qualify for a gift or grant. Apply for everything! They all add up! To get a list of any possible gifts or grants available to apply for, visit your school guidance counselor or local library or bookstore. You'll find more books than you can imagine on this area. You can also go to your Internet search engine and look under "paying for college."

Government Education Plans

The first plan we'll cover is the **Coverdell ESA (formerly known as the Education IRA).** At the writing of this book, the Coverdell ESA had just been improved. However, it is important for you to research this area, as rules can change year to year. Therefore, this information could be outdated by the time you read this book. However, I still feel it's important to cover and at least give you some of the basics to see if it might be an option for your student.

First, let's discuss the difference between "qualified" and "non-qualified" investment programs.

Notes:

_____

_____

_____

_____

A qualified program means that the account grows tax-deferred. As you invest money and it earns interest, dividends or capital gains, you would normally have to pay taxes on the interest earned. In a qualified account, the investment can grow and earn interest without any taxation on the earnings as long as the money remains in the account.

Non-qualified simply means it is not a tax-deferred approved savings plan and, therefore, you would have to pay taxes in the year you earned the interest. Obviously, if you get to keep 100% of the earnings in the plan and not be required to use some of the earnings to pay the tax, it allows the account to grow and accumulate much quicker when tax-deferred.

Just about any investment can be utilized as a Coverdell ESA. Many times I hear people refer to an IRA as if it is an investment in and of itself. I might say, how do you have your IRA invested and the answer is "Merrill Lynch" or "Standard Federal Bank." This tells me what institution holds my IRA, but not how it's invested.

When you enter a bank and say you would like an IRA, the banker will most likely put your money into a Certificate of Deposit, or a "CD." Then they have you sign a piece of paper saying you want your CD to be an IRA. If you go to a financial planner, they might put you in a mutual fund or stock. Then you sign a piece of paper saying that you want the fund or stock to be your IRA.

A Coverdell ESA works the same way. You decide how much risk or how little risk you wish to take on the investment and then invest the money appropriately.

Notes:

_____

_____

_____

_____

A Coverdell ESA can be opened for as little as $25 per month. Therefore, most anyone can participate. Remember, however, your maximum investment each year cannot exceed $2,000 per child. If you exceed the maximum, there is a 6% penalty tax for over funding.

Not everyone can use a Coverdell ESA. The government has determined if you earn more than a certain amount, you cannot participate. If you are a single filer, you begin losing your ability to invest in an education IRA at an adjusted gross income of $95,000. If you are married filing jointly, you begin losing your ability to invest this way when your adjusted gross is $190,000 or more.

Some final points on Coverdell ESA's are that you cannot use them in conjunction with any state savings plans (such as 529 plans, we'll discuss these later).

- Distributions
  1. Part principal, part interest each year.
  2. If expenses exceed the total amount distributed in one year, all earnings are excluded from the beneficiaries' income.
  3. If expenses are less than distributed amount, earnings are taxed as income to beneficiary and a 10% penalty tax is assessed.
- Eligible Institutions
  Providing Bachelors degree or graduate-level or professional degree.
- Transferability
  Must be child from same family

Notes:

_____

_____

_____

_____

529 Plans

A 529 plan is an investment plan operated by a state designed to help families save for future college costs. There are two general types of 529 plans: prepaid programs and savings programs. Prepaid plans usually have more restrictions on usage within or without of your state of residency. However, the savings programs open the door for a wider base of use. For now, we will focus more on the savings programs.

There are four main advantages to 529 plans. First, you receive some tremendous tax breaks. Your investment grows tax-free for as long as your investment stays in the plan. When distributions are made for the beneficiary's (usually a child) college costs, the distribution is federally tax-free.

Secondly, you the donor stay in full control of the assets invested in the plan! This is a big change from the old Uniform Gift To Minors (UGMA) accounts. UGMA accounts provided a way to contribute money into a child's name. Parents usually did this as a college investment. It would also mean the earnings on the investment were taxed at the child's rate. However, once the money was placed in the child's name, it belonged to the child. At their eighteenth birthday, they now had full control of the money.
If a shiny new corvette was more to their liking than a college education, there was nothing the parent could do about it.

In the 529 plan the named beneficiary of the account (the child) at no time has any rights to the assets. You get to call the shots and determine when and how they may use the money for schooling. If your child never goes to college, you can reclaim the funds but you will have a 10%

Notes:

_____

_____

_____

_____

penalty and taxes due on the earnings portion of the account (maybe that's still better than the Corvette).

Third, a 529 plan can be rather easy to administer. In most cases, you can control the investment vehicle used. Therefore, you can simply choose an investment as conservative or aggressive as you wish. Once invested, if chosen wisely, they require little or no management.

Finally, everyone is eligible for a 529 plan. Parents and grandparents face no limitations to contribute based on their current earned income. Each account for the beneficiary can accept up to $200,000 in contributions.

You are not restricted to use the 529 plan of a certain state. You are free to invest wherever you find the best option for your specific needs.

Use the Internet

One of the websites I can recommend is www.savingforcollege.com. It is a wealth of information on Coverdell ESA's as well as 529 plans. You can also enter any search engine, and simply type in "college funding" or "college financing," and you'll find more sites to visit than you could imagine.

Other ways to make college possible

I have met with people in the early days of my financial planning career who were distraught over how to fund their kid's college education. I would hear them project college costing $80,000, and they saw no way to cover such an expense. Then, in reviewing their finances, I note how

Notes:

_____

_____

_____

_____

they have a $60,000 to $80,000 home equity loan. When asked why the loan is there, I would hear a number of different reasons. Some of them would be logical and justify the loan. Many, however, had tapped the loans to buy a Cadillac Escalade, or to satisfy their middle-age crisis, they bought a Jaguar. Sometimes the loan paid for a built-in swimming pool or the lake home they've always dreamed of.

Sometimes, it's really a matter of priorities. If funding a college education is truly important, then what are you willing to give up in exchange for it? It's time to be bluntly honest with ourselves, Mom and Dad.

Whoever said they had to go to Harvard?

I personally believe the best path for "MOST" high school graduates and their parents is to have the child stay home for the first two years and go to a local junior college or local university.

My daughter Kelly, went away to college her first year out of high school. As wonderful and well adjusted as she was, and is, she was still only 18. Have you ever stopped to reflect on what you were like at 18 versus 20 or 21? What a difference! The degree of maturing that takes place in those few years is an easily recognizable difference by most anyone.

Kelly went to a Christian college the first year that was somewhat stricter than what she had planned on. Not only that, it was her first time away from home for an extended period of time. At times she would call home crying about how she hated it there. Once, she called to say the

Notes:

_____

_____

_____

_____

school had her in the Dean's office for climbing through a window after curfew for freshman. I'll spare you the tales of her freshman year.

The next year, Kelly stayed home and studied at the local junior college. Kelly herself will tell you that it was the best decision she could have made. She needed that one extra year to regroup and make some big decisions about who she is and what she wants to do with the rest of her life. This year, she will once again go away to Palm Beach Atlantic University in West Palm Beach, Florida. However, this time she and her parents feel she is ready.

Too many times, parents feel it's the "thing to do" to send their kids to a school away from home in their first year. I mean, isn't that what all "good" parents do? I believe it's far more important (and the best way parents can help their child) to assess the gifts and maturity of their student, as well as the necessity of leaving home in order to go to school.

For most, there are many local universities and junior colleges available in your area. Besides, if you heard some of the stories Connie and I had about what many 18- and 19-year-olds are doing outside the college classroom their first two years, it would make all parents think twice about sending the kids away to school during that time.

Please don't take this advice as a blanket statement of what's right for all students. Many students are ready to leave home and go away to school at 18. They have a firm goal and plan for their life and feel the need to attend a certain school beginning their freshman year. However, consider sending your kids to local colleges for the first two years. Then, when they have two additional years of maturity, they can transfer to a college or university of their choice.

Notes:

_____

_____

_____

_____

What about the degree? Isn't the school the degree comes from of major importance? In most cases no, in some cases, yes. However, going to a local college for the first two years does not dictate where the degree is eventually earned. I've never heard of a case where someone went in for a job interview and was asked, "I see your degree is from Harvard. However, where did you spend your first two years?"

Finally, the cost of school becomes far more attainable. Assume your child attends a local college costing them between $2,000 and $6,000 each of the first two years. Using an average, that would be about $$4,000 per year or $8,000 for the first two. This is, of course, assuming they don't qualify for any gifts, grants or scholarships. Then add the last two years, say at an average cost of $20,000 each year, and the total cost of education falls from $80,000 to $48,000. While this is still a large bill, and to some overwhelming, it could now make a home equity loan more feasible. Also, if your student had to borrow money, that's $32,000, he or she doesn't have to pay back. If the cost is still too high, most people live within driving distance of a four-year college or university. Your child can always commute and drop the four-year cost to around $20,000 total ($8,000 for two years at junior college and $12,000 for two years at a university). These numbers are strictly for illustration and certainly as the years go by, will rise. The ideas, however, remain the same.

But, Curt, I don't want to borrow ANY money! Then it's time to begin investigating other possibilities. They will all require time, effort and education, but it can be done.

Notes:

_____

_____

_____

_____

One way that Robert Kiyosaki and others like Robert Allen, author of "No Money Down" teach as a means to fund college is to do through real estate. This requires some time to learn about it, but my understanding is that the basics are really quite simple. I myself am not invested in single-family homes. However, I do have a number of investments in commercial real estate. In single-family homes, I have both read about and have friends, who have done just what I'm sharing with you. The idea is to search the market place to find some foreclosed property. Remember, you're not foreclosing on them, the bank already has. You're simply helping them out of a jam. If you could buy a house worth $150,000 for $135,000 and put about $2,000 of repairs into it, and sell it yourself for $148,000, you would make a profit of $11,000. Do that once each year that your child is in college and you've provided $44,000 toward her education.

I admit, you must dedicate yourself to studying a bit and learning about this process, but it could be everything you need. If not real estate, be creative. Where there's a will, there is always a way.

Uncle Sam can help!

You may be thinking at this point that I still don't understand how poor you are. I know this, my parents, Marvin and Norah were unable to offer me anything financially toward college. They were, as far as I'm concerned, the finest parents I could have asked for. However, rich they were not. When each of their four kids graduated high school, the folks said we love you and will do anything we can, but financially, we can't help at all. They were living paycheck to paycheck.

Notes:

_____

_____

_____

_____

191

I was determined to make it through college. I had a dream in my heart and was bound and determined not to let money stop me. Two month after my high school graduation, I got a job a Chrysler Corporation. My Uncle Leo was a plant manager and made it possible. I decided I would work for a year and save my money. Then I'd quit and go to school for a year. Then go back to work and then school again for a year. I was told by many of the men at Chrysler that I'd never leave and would end up a "lifer" there. At the end of my year I quit and went to my first year of school.

However, Connie would tell you I live in a microwave world. When I want something, I seldom have great patience in waiting. I must tell you, some of the toughest lessons in life for me involved patience. At the end of my first year, I just knew this brainstorm of mine wasn't going to work. So, what did I do? I joined the Navy.

At the time, 1973, the Vietnam War was winding down and the GI Bill was still in place. The GI Bill would help me pay for my college degree. It worked! After the Navy, I graduated two years later. Wait a minute you say; I thought you only had one year of education in before joining the Navy. So how did you graduate in just two more years after the Navy? The reason is that I had some training while in the Navy that was in line with my degree. In addition, while I was sailing around the ocean, I subscribed to correspondence courses that also were accredited and accepted by the school I planned to attend after my honorable discharge. I literally completed another year of college while in the Navy and serving my country!

As I write this chapter, I am sitting at the window of my hotel room in San Diego, California. I came out for a few days of business. On the

Notes:

_____

_____

_____

_____

flight here, I sat next to a man who had been a paratrooper in the Army. He told me that the military now has a savings plan where you can save money for college. He is now out of the Army and attending a University in Ohio in the field of computer technology; and guess who's paying for it? That's right, the Army.

If a child truly has a dream in his or her heart and a passion to achieve something in life, a lack of money will never stop them. Sometimes, that's where the best lessons are learned and positive attitudes are developed. Dream on, America! Where there's a will, there is always a way!

Notes:

_____

_____

_____

_____

CHAPTER TWELVE

TEACHING YOUR CHILDREN ABOUT MONEY

God truly blessed me when he gave me Connie as my wife. When it comes to knowing what to do as our children grew, she was the one with all the common sense. I unfortunately was the one who reacted to circumstances with, *"I'm going to kill them!"* Then Connie would calm me down and help me think through the issues and together, we would come up with what was the best approach. As a result, I couldn't be prouder of the children we have raised. They bring us joy, happiness, and, yes, from time to time still some grief. But, I wouldn't trade the moments good and bad with our kids for anything.

The reason I mention this is because I am NOT an expert on raising children. I'm quite a ways off from that. Nor, am I a child psychiatrist. Therefore, as I write this chapter, I do so humbly and with no intention of convincing you I have all the answers. However, I do have some ideas and thoughts I believe may be helpful as you raise your children from the financial perspective.

Learning how to handle money has never been more important for our children than today. By now, you know that I come from the Detroit area. When I was growing up, the talk was all about getting your education and then going to work for one of the Big Three automakers.

Notes:

_____

_____

_____

_____

When I was younger, I heard many people say that my goal in life should be to work for a company like General Motors, Ford or Chrysler. The plan was to work there for 30 plus years and then retire happily ever after with a big fat pension. Those days are gone! Long gone!

Today, the idea of working your whole career in one spot is almost a fairy tale. The major companies in America don't want an employee to reach pension qualification. It's far too expensive for them to administer the pension plan and even more expensive to fund it. Therefore, if they make sure no one gets past 20 to 25 years, they can control or even eliminate that overhead.

It is now all about 401-K plans and IRA's and people planning their own retirement. The only problem with that is, who's going to teach the American worker how to build his or her own pension plan.

I don't know about you, but my parents taught me very little about money because they never had much themselves. They weren't the best money managers, so whom could I turn to, to learn. I hope this book has helped you learn a great deal about money matters and I hope you be determined to teach your kids these truths so they can have it even better for their future.

In the last chapter, we spoke quite a bit about college and the value of it as well as making sure we use it properly. When we go to college, we go to learn a career and hopefully to learn how to make a good income in the process. The key once we graduate then is to learn what to do with the money we make. This is where most people get in trouble and get off to a poor start. They never developed the right habits or attitudes about money. Well educated doesn't mean we have our financial act together.

Notes:

_____

_____

_____

_____

We must learn how to make money work for us, rather than just us learning how to make money. If we don't, the Bible clearly states in Proverbs what can happen as we borrow. We become a slave to our lenders. We spend the rest of our life working for everyone but ourselves.

I have mentioned several times throughout this book about one of my favorite authors, Robert Kiyosaki. I again urge you to read all of his books and just as important, pass them on to your kids. In one of his books, he mentions a statement his father once made. His father said, "My banker has never asked to see my report card. He only wants to see my financial statements!" You have already learned how to read a financial statement through this book and Roberts' if you've read them. Now, make sure you teach your children how to read them. Draw out the boxes and teach your children the difference between an asset and a liability. Draw out the arrows; it will give them a great start.

Kiyosaki also markets a game on www.richdad.com called "Cash Flow for Kids." It's a great game and learning tool that I highly recommend. It teaches the fact "you get rich at home, not at work." What's he mean by this. The key is not how much you earn at work. Rather, it's what you do with the money once you get it home. Where does the paycheck go? Those decisions are the real key to financial freedom.

A Few More Ideas

Many people ask, "Is an allowance OK?" The answer is that it depends on how it is given or earned. If you simply decide that your children need some spending money and therefore hand them $10 per week, you are basically teaching them to believe in a welfare system. If you ever

Notes:

_____

_____

_____

_____

have a need for money, honey, someone will always be there to help you out. Then we wonder why so many adults are mad when the Government isn't taking care of them.

I feel there should be some things that we expect our children to do as a member of the household, that they don't get paid for. Things like making their beds, picking up after themselves, putting things away after they're done with them and carrying their dishes to the sink after dinner. However, there can also be some jobs assigned along the way. This way, they can earn the money they make and learn that free handouts don't exist in real life. What you deem as non-paying events and paying events is up to each home to decide for themselves. In our house, Kris gets paid for mowing the lawn, weeding, edging and blowing the snow. Kelly cleans the house from top to bottom as her pay. It goes way beyond just picking up after themselves.

Not too long back, I decided to finish our basement. We mapped out a great layout with a kitchen, bath, rec. area and, of course, the big screen TV complete with surround sound. I was torn, as to pay someone else to do it or do it myself. Financially, I actually would be ahead to pay someone else based on time demands. However, after much consideration and thought, I felt it would be a great opportunity to hire Kris and provide him a way to earn some extra money (what I was really interested in was time with my son).

I presented the idea and terms to Kris. After some thought, he accepted the job. At some of the craziest times, I had moments with my son that could not be predicted or replaced. Once, we had set a goal to finish wiring the kitchen area complete with garbage disposal and microwave. It took longer than we thought (it always does), but at the end, we braced

Notes:

_____

_____

_____

_____

ourselves as I had Kris hit the circuit breaker. Would it all work? Are we the very essence of Mr. Fix-it? Are we the men of the house? He hit the switch. We then took a shop light and one by one placed it in every plug. We tried every switch and YES! Everything worked perfectly. We let out a scream, hugged each other as only two grizzly bears could and marched up the basement stairs singing "We Are The Champions!" Some other times I wouldn't trade for the world were simple trips to Home Depot. We would end up talking about school, girls, life and what ever else came to mind. Hiring someone else to do the basement could have been the most expensive thing I had ever done. Now all we have to do is finish it!

OK, the kids are generating money. Now the most critical part once again presents itself. Are you teaching your kids what to do with the money once they earn it? I believe this requires a dedicated time to sit and talk with your child.

When the time was right for Kelly, I had mentioned to her to block some time in her day for us to talk about the money she was now making. She groaned slightly at the thought of sitting and talking about such a boring subject. What happened, I could have never predicted. Kelly had forgotten about our set meeting time and had invited over her friend Carrie. When I brought up the fact it was meeting time, she proceeded to moan and groan about how she and Carrie had made plans and that the timing was bad. I reminded her of her commitment to me and invited Carrie to join us at the kitchen table. Begrudgingly, the girls sat down, promptly propped their face in their hands and began to look immediately bored.

Notes:

_____

_____

_____

_____

As I began to talk, I started drawing out the income statement and balance sheet. The girls were starting to understand some of the key principles and I saw them just slightly begin to perk up and show an interest. When they saw the arrow circling from the asset column back into the income column, they said, "Well, why doesn't everyone understand this?"

I then went on and ran some numbers of what saving $25 per month would do for them over the next 40 years. Now the excitement began! They perked up big time, and began talking about how rich they would be and all the stuff they were going to buy with their newfound wealth.

If you refer back to chapter 3, you'll remember a chart on Procrastinator Pete and Eager Eddie. That chart indicated what $83.33 per month could do when you start investing early. This could perhaps be helpful to you as you strive to teach your children the value of sound financial management.

As Kelly began earning money, I made it imperative that with each of her first few paychecks, we should sit down and divide out where the money was to go. It is critical that your children learn to make the decisions about the money before they even cash their check. Once I had worked with her a few times, she had it down and was able to go forward on her own.

Today, Kelly is almost 21. While she leaves for school in about another week, it was thrilling to me to watch her for the last year at home manage her money. Each payday, she would walk in to our home office and say, "Here you go, Dad." And hand me a check made out to her investment plan. I haven't had to beg her or plead with her; it was ingrained from

Notes:

_____

_____

_____

_____

the very beginning. I have had the same talks with my son Kris. He is quite convinced that he will be financially free by the age of 30.

About four months ago, Connie was off with some girlfriends and the kids and I were home. Kelly's friend, Jen, came by, and I offered to take the two of them along with Kris to Chili's for dinner. Being young adults now, and never passing on free food, they jumped at the opportunity.

While at dinner, Kelly looked at me and said; "Hey Dad, teach Jen all that stuff you've taught Kris and me about financial freedom." I took a napkin and drew out the income statement and balance sheet. Within 10 minutes, the whole table was bouncing with excitement. All four of us had a great time. That night, as I lay in bed with the lights out, I reflected on the lesson at dinner and how my children were helping me teach their friend about handling money and financial freedom. A slow but very satisfying grin formed on my face. I thanked the Lord for the opportunity and then had a very good night's sleep.

There's More Off The Top Than Investing

Imagine a Mama pig that has just had some piglets. The piglets are hungry and depending on Mama to feed them. Of course being a mother, Mama is building up the nourishment to feed her piglets. However, let's assume Mama pig decides not to feed her kids. What would eventually happen to her? She would explode!

In the great design of our world and life, I believe it was meant to be that we always be looking for ways to give something back for the general good of people rather than to always be taking and taking. I feel it is

Notes:

_____

_____

_____

_____

important that the first proceeds off the top of our income go to our church, place of worship or charity. This helps round out our life and provide us what we all deep down desire, to serve people. Imagine the ways that your tithe or donation can be multiplied to help tens, hundreds, maybe even thousands of people who may be less fortunate than us.

There is an old saying, what goes around, comes around. If you never spend any of your time giving back, I highly doubt that you will consistently succeed for any period of time. You may be successful for a short time. But, ultimately, it will come back to hurt you. I'm not saying this is always financial. In our early days of marriage, Connie and I went through some tough times financially. However, we had wonderful healthy children. Though broke and financially limited, we continued to give during that time. Could it be that our blessings at that time were in our children? The ways you can be blessed for giving do not always come through financial rewards. I have found in my own life, that my greatest rewards come when my focus is on how I can best serve others, rather than always looking for ways to serve myself.

Happiness does not come from making more money.

Another lessoned I've learned along the way is that happiness does not come from making more money. In reality, I have found that if my whole focus is on making more money, I tend to get grouchy and ornery. I carry a much higher degree of stress in my life, which results in more health problems and a poor family and spiritual life.

When I allow money to simply be a by-product of what I do, then my focus is more on what I do, what I enjoy and serving others. No longer

Notes:

_____

_____

_____

_____

do I carry the financial stress and I'm free to do what truly brings me joy and contentment. Amazingly, money always seems to take care of itself.

Finally, I would like to address helping our children by focusing on their mental well being as well as financial. I would urge parents reading this book to formulate a strong positive self-image in their children. It doesn't matter how they look, if they are popular or not, or how great or weak of a personality they may carry. Your child has the ability to be an awesome asset to society and a productive and happy person. It all begins early right inside the home.

I have mentioned it before, but identifying your child's gifts is a critical part of building self-esteem. When we are younger, we all slowly but surely identify what we excel at and what we don't. We receive accolades and compliments on things we do, even though we aren't seeking the compliments. Unfortunately, for many, we never really know how to identify what our gifts are. By the time we truly recognize our gifts, we may be close to or in our retirement. If that describes you, it's not too late. Remember Colonel Sanders, founder of Kentucky Fried Chicken, didn't start KFC until he was in his 60's. However, if we can help our children recognize their gifts early in life, they will have a huge head start toward "beginning" their life and career headed in the right direction rather than spending the first 20,30 or 40 years of their adult life finding where they belong.

As you know, I spent 12 years in radio broadcasting. Through accolades and compliments I received as a youth, I knew I had a good personality and a love for the spotlight. One night, I was between my second and third year of high school. I was pondering on what I would do with my

Notes:

203

life. Suddenly, a disc jockey began to talk on the radio station I was listening to and it hit me. "Wow," I said! "I could be a disc jockey. It would be a really "cool" way to make a living." I was missing one key ingredient. I didn't have a voice for radio. I ended up in the sales department and did very well. I was the top salesman and eventually was promoted to sales manager at the age of 24. After a couple of years of successful selling, I decided that I should now be a general manager of a station (I know, I had a really big head). I began reading Broadcasting Magazine and found a station in St. Louis, MO looking for a GM. I applied for the job and amazingly got it. At the age of 26, to my knowledge, I was the youngest GM in the top 20 markets in radio. There was only one problem. As good as I was at selling radio, I wasn't gifted in the area of administration. I felt I did a very good job while serving as GM. However, I was miserable. Why? I wasn't using my true gifts at that time. I was doing a good job, but not a great job, which is where much of our self-esteem comes from.

I left radio and went into financial planning. I was back in sales and felt more at home there. Things began to happen in my new career. I was doing so well selling, that they promoted me to a manager position. I was now in charge of the office I began working at. One problem, I was once again in administration. I eventually left that company to form my own. C. Curtis & Associates first opened its doors on October 15, 1986. Each time I would add personnel and start to grow, things would slow down. Whenever it was just me selling, things would get better.

It wasn't until about three years ago that I finally discovered what my gifted areas were. My predominant gift is teaching. I believe that's why I was always successful at selling. The best salespeople are good teachers.

Notes:

_____

_____

_____

_____

I was approached at my home church in Plymouth, Michigan, NorthRidge Church about teaching a class. I accepted and received many compliments how much people enjoyed the class. Before long, I was being asked to teach many different classes. Each time, the same thing happened. People would come up and say how much they learned. It would be easy for someone to get a big head at this point. However, I was given the gift of teaching. I didn't earn it, deserve it or ask for it, it was a gift. How then can you get a big head about something you had nothing to do with? Rather, it is important to use the gift to help others.

Shortly after teaching in church, it hit me that if I have the gift of teaching others, why not begin to hold financial seminars. I was scared to death to make the investment in my first seminar. I had about 125 people attend, and at the end, all of them were very enthusiastic! Many people came up to Connie or to me and said this had been the best seminar they had ever attended. Probably my greatest compliment came from one senior lady who I would guess was about 85. She said; "This is the first seminar on money I have ever attended, that I didn't fall asleep!"

Finally, I decided that if I spend my whole day teaching people with money how to manage their assets, what about those who have little or no money? Who's helping them? The answer is not many. You see, financial planners want to speak to people with money to invest. That's how they make their living. So to meet with someone who has nothing to invest, would financially be a waste of time.

The Financial Freedom Education Institute was born in 2000. Our company's goal and mission is to help those in debt, not only become

Notes:

_____

_____

_____

_____

debt free, but to become financially free at the same time, by teaching them the basics of money management and attitudes about money.

Think of how great of an advantage your children will have when you help them discover where they happen to be gifted. Focus on their strengths, not their weaknesses. This builds self-esteem and hopefully they will find where they would be more than good, they'd be great!

Talk to your kids about retiring at age 30 or 40. This may sound absurd, but it actually puts their wheels in motion to be smart about financial matters from the very beginning. Once they think it's possible, they will then be willing to think of ways to make it happen.

I believe one of the biggest reasons young people in America don't begin to invest early is because 60-65 seems so far off they get the attitude of "I've got plenty of time to invest. Right now, I just want to have fun!" They then begin to proceed to form all of the bad habits that become a weight and burden to them later in life and can make it extremely difficult to change. They ultimately become a slave to their lenders.

Moms and Dads, you will create a legacy for generations to follow you. It will either be a legacy of debt and bondage or wealth and financial freedom. What will you pass on?

Notes:

CHAPTER THIRTEEN

FINDING AN ADVISOR TO TRUST IN

When I first started in the financial planning field almost 21 years ago, I had every intention of being the best planner anyone had ever been to. I knew I was bringing honesty and integrity to the table for each client I would meet. However, the best of intentions does not mean that I was actually the best or giving the best advice. At the time I was giving the advice, it was the best I knew of and had to offer. You see the key words there are the "best I could offer." Just how good can my advice be when I have only been in the business for six months? I was telling people exactly what I had been trained to tell them by the people who trained me. I was moving forward based only on my belief in my superiors and what I was trained to say.

When the market is rolling along well as it did from 1988 – 1999, any advice can turn out to be good advice. However, when things turn bad as they did in 2000 – 2002, then the right advice becomes critical. Having an experienced advisor becomes more important than ever.

So, if you're just starting out on your venture to build your asset column and net worth, how do you find a highly experienced advisor to help you? Unfortunately, you probably won't! Unless you are a relative or closely connected to someone who currently works with such an advisor, the truly experienced and knowledgeable ones may be out of reach. Many advisors have requirements for them to work with you.

Notes:

_____

_____

_____

_____

Requirements could be a minimum size investment portfolio, a minimum net worth or a certain age group.

For people just starting out, there are plenty of advisors willing to help you. However, they are usually newer in the industry and fighting to work their way up the ladder to deal with bigger clientele. This usually means less experience. That's not necessarily bad, the important thing is for you to recognize they are newer and your role in the team is very important.

In this chapter, I will first discuss two types of financial advisors. I will tell you what to look for in an advisor and give you some criteria for your search. I will also tell you, based on your financial situation, which of the two advisors you can expect to work with. After discussing advisors, I will give you my thoughts on some basic principals of investing.

All True Financial Planners Are Strategists

All true financial planners are strategists. Their job is to help you identify where you're currently at, help you determine where you want to go financially and by what time or age you want to get there. They would involve questions such as:

- At what age would like to retire?
- If you were at your desired retirement age today, how much income in today's dollars would you need to be happily retired?
- If you were to die, Mr. Jones, Mrs. Jones would you want to go back to work or still be able to stay home with the children?
- Do you want to cover your children's college? How much of it?

Notes:

_____

_____

_____

_____

These are some questions you should expect to hear from a good financial planner. If you go in to see a "financial planner," and he or she immediately recommends that you buy or invest in something that day, you need to keep looking. Any one who calls himself or herself a financial planner but doesn't ask planning questions, is in reality, just a salesperson. They only care about a commission and not truly planning your future. There are four things every planner should do.

- Identify your desires both present and future.
- Plan a path to follow to get you there.
- Help implement the plan.
- Guide you in making decisions based on your goals.

There are three main types of planners. Which one you work with depends on your current circumstances.

Foundational Planner

- *Works with all income and investment levels.*

Foundational planners are sometimes but not always newer in the business. They are striving to build their foundation of clients. They also are usually the ones who have been trained to help you by asking the right questions.

Notes:

_____

_____

_____

_____

- *Identifies point "A" and desired point "B."*

They definitely help you identify where you're at today and help you decide where you'd like to someday be. Then, they tell you what you must do to get there.

- *Help's find cash flow to implement plan.*

A good foundational planner will also be able to help you identify where you may be spending or letting money slip through your fingers. By tweaking here and there, he or she can come up with money you never knew you were wasting and help direct it into your retirement. Many of these ideas have already been covered in this book.

- *Help's identify risk tolerance level.*

Everyone has a certain risk tolerance level when investing. I usually ask my clients to pick a number from one to ten. Ten would mean willingness to take risk. One meaning no risk at all could be tolerated.

- *Help's identify investment choices.*

Then the planner will help direct you to investments that would meet your goals and whenever possible, do so within your risk tolerance level.

- *Mostly works with insurance and investments.*

Most foundational-planners work with investments and insurance. Part of the reason for this, is that the commissions on the investments by

Notes:

_____

_____

_____

_____

someone investing $50 - $100 per month are at best, $2.50 to $5.00 per month. I think you would agree, this income would not be sufficient to support any one individual, much less a family.

However, most people just starting out in investments are almost always underinsured. More often than not, they need the insurance the planner is representing. The combination of commissions on both the investments and insurance, make a reasonable living possible.

- *Commissioned based income.*

Most foundational planners work solely off a commission income. Please don't begrudge them the ability to earn an income for their family. I think you'll find 80% of all planners are striving to do the right thing for their clients. Unfortunately, it's the other 20% that hurt the reputation of all the good planners.

How can you know if the planner you are talking to is in the 80% of good ones? Get references to start. Also, as you begin your search, ask friends and family who they use. How long have they used them? Are they really happy with the planner? If the person giving you the referral hasn't worked with the planner at least three years, I would keep looking. It takes at least three years to be able to form a good opinion of the planner's abilities, advice and service.

Foundational Planners Are Not Money Managers

Often, a financial planner will lead the new client to believe that they will manage their portfolio for them. It goes something like this: *Mr. Jones, I see you've not been happy with the returns your portfolio has*

Notes:

_____

_____

_____

_____

produced in the past. What you need, to be able to sleep better at night, is to have someone more closely manage your investments. Right now, you are in what is called a "buy and hold" strategy. You buy a fund and then just take the ride. If the investment goes up, you're up. If the investment goes down, you're down. No one, Mr. Jones, is watching your money!

If given the chance, Mr. Jones, I will not only help you realign your investments so that they are in the best place. I will also help watch your money and make recommendations throughout the year to always make sure you are well diversified and balanced and protect your investments against downside risk.

This sounds really good to most investors. Why? They don't want to be bothered with having to worry about or manage their investments. The only problem is that a foundational planner won't do any of the above. Don't get me wrong; they can still be a good planner and advisor. They just don't have, nor will they make, time to watch your money. They can't watch your money!

Think about it. How does a foundational planner make their income? They make their income through commissions. Again, there is nothing wrong with that. As I said, everyone needs to support his or her family. As long as they are doing it honestly and with integrity, commissions are deserved and more than fair. The thing you must guard against is falling for the "sales pitch" above.

For a commission-based planner to make a good living, the key is how many clients can they see in a day? Almost 100% of their income comes right up front as you make your initial investment. The commissions

Notes:

_____

_____

_____

_____

they receive each year after the first are extremely low and would make it very difficult to support themselves and depend on.

As soon as you leave the planner's office and the next client walks in, you need to ask yourself, "Who's watching my money while he's speaking to the next client?"

I'm sharing this with you, because I used to be solely a commissioned based planner for many years. I had the greatest intentions and truly desired to serve those I met with. However, no matter how good my intentions were, I just couldn't keep up with the demands of following each person's account and calling him regularly to suggest changes he may need to be make.

If you are a new investor, a foundational planner can at least help you identify your goals and proper places for you to invest your money to get started. He will be there in the event you need to call and discuss questions or more detailed planning ideas. A foundational planner is the advisor, for those just beginning to seek the help they need. You must remember that it is expected of you to be pro-active in managing your assets in the early days.

Until you reach around $10,000 to $25,000 of investments, I would recommend you find a good investment and just keep adding to it. There isn't much to manage and the name of the game here is to just keep socking it away. If you're investing in the market, dollar cost averaging (discussed earlier) will handle the management of your money.

Notes:

_____

_____

_____

_____

Once you reach the level of investments noted in the previous paragraph, I then feel you should revisit with your planner to make sure your diversification is established in line with your wiliness to take risk.

Once your investments reach the $50,000 range, I recommend you begin to search for a "money manager" to help manage your portfolio. Obviously, if you desire to study and learn the field of investing and do it on your own, I advocate that as well. However, if you think you're going to manage the money effectively on a part-time basis while running a business, career and family, please see a money manager!

Fee-Based-Money-Manager Planner

This type of planner does most of what the foundational planner does, with the exception of the last few points above. Fee-based-money-manager planners themselves are broken into three types.

1. Fees for managing assets.
2. Fees for time spent with you or
3. Fees and commissions.

First, let's look at the fee for managing assets planner. Here are some of the differences and what you can expect form this type of planner.

- *Works with higher net-worth clients.*

This form of fee-based planner may charge nothing for the meeting time you have with them. They derive their income by charging a fee for assets under management. Say you had $100,000 to invest and asked a fee-based planner to manage it for you. The typical fee today ranges

Notes:

_____

_____

_____

_____

form 1% to 3% per year of assets. That means on $100,000, your first year fee if you were paying 2% would be $2,000 for the year.

What many investors like about fee-based-money-manager planners is that there is no front-end charge. There is no early withdrawal or surrender charge. Your investment is always liquid. Finally, if your account goes up in value, the planner makes more money. However, if your account value goes down, then the planner loses money. Many investors feel that if the planner makes them money, he or she deserves a raise. If, on the other hand, he loses you money, he too would lose income. You can say then the fee-based planner has a personal interest in your success.

- *Manages investments in on-going basis.*

Unlike the foundational planner, the fee-based-money-manager planner is being paid on a regular basis for the sole purpose of "actively" managing your assets. Therefore, you should expect quality service. If you are not meeting with them at least annually and hearing from them quarterly, they aren't doing the job they are being paid for.

- *Requires minimum size investment.*

Most fee-based-money-manager planners have a minimum investment size before they will work with you. This is understandable, in that it takes just as much time to manage a $500,000 account as it does a $25,000 account. Since, they are paid by assets under management each planner will decide what their minimum account size is in order to accept your account.

Notes:

_____

_____

_____

This type of planner can perform in a way as to manage your investments. However, one word of caution! It is wise to ask this form of planner how many clients he has now and how many he plans to limit taking as clients. If he allows his client base to grow too large, then the quality of the service he provides will begin to erode.

Fee and Commission-Based Planners

These planners will represent smaller clients and larger clients. They will work with clients on a commission base for smaller amounts, and work on a fee basis with larger accounts. They will do the same type work as the foundational and fee-based-money-manager planners, except, the good ones will use outside money managers to manage the client's assets and take a smaller portion of the fee in doing so. If you ever come across a planner that says he makes both commissions and fees, that's acceptable, as long as he doesn't also tell you he will manage your money for you. He will be too busy meeting new clients and servicing others to actually manage your account. That's why he works with outside money managers who "only" manage money.

Fee-Only Planner

The fee-only planners will only charge an hourly rate for meeting and having them draw up a plan for you. They don't sell any products and they don't try to manage money. They simply charge an hourly rate to advise you. You then would implement the plan on your own based on their advice.

Fee-only planners usually charge anywhere from $150 per hour and up. Therefore, they could be a bit expensive for someone just starting out.

Notes:

_____

_____

_____

_____

This is the hardest form of planner to find in America. Virtually 99%, in my opinion, of all planners will either be foundational, fee and commission, or fee-based-money-managers.

Keys To Finding A Good Planner

The keys are really dependent on which type of planner you are looking for. If you're just getting started investing, the commission-based, fee-and-commission based planner would both be appropriate. The fee-only planner is the best if you are working your way out of debt. However, they may be too costly. As you search for a financial planner, don't be in a hurry. This is an important step. Patience will usually insure that you find the best one for you. Meet with at least three different planners in your community. This way you can get a feel for each one. Here are some other ideas of things to look for during your search

Credentials can help, but don't rely on them too much. Credentials such as CFP, CFA, ChFC, CPA, CSA, or CEP are just a few of the credentials your planner may carry. While this does not guaranty quality, honesty or integrity, it does tell you that the person you're meeting with cares enough about what they do to go forward and get some ongoing education to be the best they can be.

Time in business is something that can also give you some idea as to their experience. I feel any foundational planner should have at least three years in the industry. Though they are for those just getting started, some actual experience is still critical to good advice. I'll go to a doctor out of medical school for three years. I just don't want to be his first patient.

Notes:

_____

_____

_____

_____

Ask for references. No matter what form of planner you go to, make sure you ask for and call at least three references. You can bet he will give you three people who like him. However, you'll never believe some of the things that can come out during one of these conversations.

The very best place to begin looking for a financial planner is through other family members or close friends. Make sure they still fit the other recommendations above. However, it is a great start if they come highly referred by someone you know.

When searching for a fee-based planner or a planner to manage your money, a few more things become important as well.

What are their current assets under management? To even be considered, I would recommend they at least have 10 million dollars currently under management. Any less than that, they are still too new to that field of planning for me to recommend them. Again, experience is the most important key here.

Do they have a limit on how many clients they will manage? If so, what is it and how many do they manage now? If they don't really have a limit, then they won't be doing a very good job of watching your money. If when you ask the question, they have to think about it ever so slightly, it could mean they are making it up as they go.

If you are speaking to a planner who does both commissioned work as well as management. Who manages the money? Do they try to do it? Or, do they work with an outside money manager? You want to hear an

Notes:

_____

_____

_____

_____

outside money manager. Again, they can't be chasing the next new client for a commission and watching your investment.

The final key is to find someone you truly feel you can trust. If you don't feel you can trust them or feel good about them, move on!

I hope you're excited about your future! In the words of famous radio psychologist Dr. Laura, "Now go seize the day!"

Notes:

_____

_____

_____

_____

CHAPTER FOURTEEN

HOW I BECAME A SUCCESS

In this final chapter, I will share with you the greatest secret of my success. However, I must begin this chapter with a warning label. I have no intention of holding anything back. It is **my** story. Therefore, it may not be what you would expect. But to write it with anything less than the truth or what it is or was would be an injustice.

Depending on your background, your faith, and your upbringing, you may find some of this offensive or uncomfortable. I apologize in advance if this is the case. However, it's my story. If you would be easily offended, then please stop now and read no further. If you stop reading at this time, thank you for allowing me the privilege of sharing and having a part in your life. I trust the information provided has helped and will continue to help you find financial freedom.

Now, for those of you still with me, allow me to share something greater than financial freedom. In order to convey the secret to my success, I need to go back in time a bit.

When I was younger, I was blessed with parents who constantly encouraged me and told me how I could do most anything and someday would be a great success. I eventually began to believe it and anytime something good happened in my life I would say, "Gee, look at that, my folks must be right! Maybe I am going to be successful!" It wasn't that I

Notes:

_____

_____

_____

_____

didn't make a ton of mistakes and do things wrong, I just focused on and hung on to those things I did right.

The successes built on themselves, especially in the early years. Out of four children born to Marvin and Norah Whipple, I was the only one who finished college. It's not because I was better or smarter than my brothers and sisters, it was because I "had" to finish college. Let me explain. As I mentioned before, I had a dream in my heart that was planted when I was 16 years old. I decided that I wanted to be a disc jockey on the radio. However, then I went beyond just being a disc jockey. I also decided to own and run 14 radio stations across the United States. Why 14? At the time, it was the maximum number you could own by law. I had intended these radio stations to be such that they would have a "positive" impact on the lives of young people across America. An impact that would help kids and young adults learn and believe that they could find success and happiness in life. Hang in there: Later, I'll tell you how financial planning came into the picture.

While in college, I worked at the college radio station and the miracles began to happen. I did some on-air time and creative work with my professor, Dr. Tom Nash, at Biola University. He quickly became one of my heroes in life. Dr. Nash asked me if I would help by trying to sell some advertising time around the community to help raise money and support the station. The station only reached the students on campus so, I decided at first to stick with the local retailers interested in reaching the student body.

One day I decided to call an advertising agency in Los Angeles. Here's this tiny little school of 4,500 students, and I'm calling an ad agency with pillars and marble counters on the top floor of a Los Angeles skyscraper!

Notes:

_____

_____

_____

_____

To my amazement, I got the appointment and even more surprisingly got the account. My sales success was so great that I continued to build the revenues for our little station beyond anyone's expectations. In my senior year, I decided to approach a "real" radio station off campus about selling part-time for them. I got the job at KYMS in Santa Ana and sold so many ads that I equaled the sales of the full-timers on a part-time basis.

After graduation, I married my sweetheart, Connie Johnson, back in Michigan and we moved to California where I worked full time in radio sales. Immediately, I began meeting with a college buddy named Wally Hollis. He and I began putting together a proposal to buy and own our first station at the ripe ages of 23 and 22. We identified a station in Detroit, Michigan (I thought we'd start with a "tiny" market) that I had already spoken to the owner of and was given the impression we could buy the station for $3,500,000. In 1980, that was a bunch of money! We spent over six months preparing the presentation and plan.

There was only one problem. Where would two college grads, come up with 3.5 million dollars? According to a bank that showed any interest at all, we would have to come up with one million dollars for the down payment in order to have a chance of financing the rest. While in college, I met a guy who had an uncle in Michigan who ran a rather large drapery business. I called his uncle and asked if we could meet explaining the idea and a potential ownership position in the new station. He said he would listen. So Wally, Connie and I flew to Detroit to make our "pitch."

As we walked into the meeting, the drapery owner and his right- hand man walked into the room and were immediately set back by our

Notes:

_____

_____

_____

_____

apparent youth. By the end of the meeting, they committed $100,000 to the two young college grads! Not knowing where else to go, we asked them if they knew any other business owners that may be willing to listen to the same opportunity. They gave us the names of two brothers and a sister who owned auto parts stores in the metro area. Again, we were met with surprise at our age, but by the time we were done, they committed $300,000 to the plan. By the end of the two weeks, we had raised $500,000 of the $1,000,000 needed. However, we ran out of time and needed to get back to our jobs in L.A. We decided to come back and find the other $500,000 in two weeks.

During the two weeks in L.A., I received notice that the station we had planned to purchase was sold to Doubleday Broadcasting for 8.3 million dollars! We lost our bid.

I remained at KYMS for a while and almost immediately became sales manager. Times were good. Connie was working at Ford Aerospace in Newport Beach, and we both enjoyed a beautiful new home, more income than we could have dreamed of, a 280Z as a company car at the radio station, and did I say more money than we could have dreamed of? We were making about $75,000 per year combined. In 1980, that was a lot of money! However, the dream of developing stations having a positive impact on young people was still lingering in my heart.

I felt it was important that if I was going to run stations of my own, I better get some experience as a station manager rather than only a sales manager. I was reading Broadcasting Magazine and noticed an ad for a General Manager (GM) position at a station in the St. Louis, MO market. I was 26 years old. I didn't know it but that was considered way too young to have any hope of getting a position like that, especially in a top

Notes:

_____

_____

_____

_____

20 market. Guys my age would be lucky to get a GM job in Podunk, USA.

Still, I applied for the job. By this time, I was getting use to the shocked looks I would receive when people first met me and realized my age. Yep! I got the same look on this interview. Skipping the details, I got the job! As I said earlier, to my knowledge, I was the youngest GM in a top 20 market anywhere in the country.

Sounds like life was just too good to be true. Things were going great. I was moving up the ladder, and in my eyes, there was no stopping me.

The Bad Times Begin!

The station I took the GM job at was not one of the strongest stations in St. Louis. OK, it was pathetic! It was ranked 42 out of 42 in the St. Louis ratings. Didn't scare me though! I had just come from one of the top stations in Orange County, California, and I was so confident in my abilities by this point I knew this is where I belonged.

While I still believe I belonged there, it wasn't for the reasons I thought. I have a strong faith in God. I believe He decided it was the place where I would be allowed to learn some hard lessons. Note I said: "allowed." I don't believe that God does bad things to us. Rather, when we go our own way in life and not the way He designed for us to go, then the results of going our own way can be painful.

The first lesson I learned was that my success wasn't all up to me! The second lesson was that no matter what I felt I could achieve, I couldn't

Notes:

_____

_____

_____

_____

do it by myself. It's also, at this time, where I began to learn my lessons in financial freedom.

As Connie and I began to look for our new home in St. Louis, we settled on one across the Mississippi River in Belleville, Illinois. It was a gorgeous house that, frankly, we didn't need but fell in love with. It was more than we could afford at the time. However, I had been promised bonuses on any business generated above the current cash flow of the station and just knew I would have the station "rockin' and rollin'" in no time at all. So, I bought the house. The station never took off the way I had planned. Income was still not up to par and Connie had just given birth to our daughter, Kelly. As parents, we felt strongly about the importance of Connie being a full-time mom and, therefore, went from the two big incomes in California to just the one small one in St. Louis, and a HUGE mortgage on our new home. The home that I felt would be the envy of our friends became our most humiliating and humbling embarrassment. We purchased the home in 1981, and if you're old enough, you'll remember the double-digit inflation and interest rates back at that time. Our home mortgage was at a very high interest rate and resulted in outrageous payments each month. As I mentioned earlier, we lived in a "palace" with virtually no furniture. We lived in a fish bowl, as we also couldn't afford drapes.

I began to come home from work each day and find Connie sitting on the love seat (the only piece of furniture we had outside of the kitchen and bedroom), crying because that day she had received five phone calls from creditors demanding payments on the credit cards.

Notes:

_____

_____

_____

_____

I knew something had to be done!

Pressures were beginning to grow. The station was not performing as well as I had planned and the owners were beginning to put the squeeze on me to put more and more "garbage" on the air in order to make more money. It was about that time, that I had an old friend come by and offer to sell me some life insurance. Not knowing I didn't have a dime to put toward it, he made his best pitch. This was "cool" life insurance to me called Universal Life. It was brand new at the time, and you actually could make money, I was told, and build your financial future by owning it. I asked my friend how much he made by selling it and then asked if they were hiring part-time sales people. I got the job part-time and immediately found some small success. We began paying off some bills and eventually I was offered a full-time job in life insurance sales. I had to do something to stop the financial pain and free my wife from the creditors. I was getting the squeeze from the owners at the station and decided it was time to move on and go where I felt I could support the family.

I'll never forget the day I came home from the radio station with the decision to enter the life insurance business full-time. I don't ever recall crying so hard and shedding so many tears. The dream, for now, had died!

Too much more of my story, I'm afraid, would cause great pain for you to read...in more ways than one. I quickly went from life insurance sales to financial planning and in 1986, began my own financial planning firm C. Curtis & Associates. Each step along the way has been filled with more failures and some successes as well.

Notes:

_____

_____

_____

_____

The point to all of this is that I found, in my own strength, I am very limited. No matter how good I think I am or how bad, there had to be more to life than just money and climbing the corporate ladder. I always felt that the more money I made, the greater a success I would become. The bigger my house, the fancier the car, the grander the trips and vacations, the more of a success I would be. But what happens when I die? Do I take it with me? Is life about how much money I can accumulate? Or, is there more?

I by no means have ever been financially rich as most would see it. Compared to modern-day athletes and movie stars and large corporate executives, I was a little guy. Oh, but how I wanted to swim with the big fish. I wanted to swim with them so bad, I was willing to ruin my life, and the lives of the ones I loved the most, trying to get it.

As a financial planner, I have sat with people who were multi-millionaires to those totally broke, and realized they could be equally unhappy, regardless of their level of income or position. As a matter of fact, in many cases, I found the wealthy ones tended to have less happiness than the ones without money. I've known friends who were well off financially and yet still miserable. If money buys happiness, why are so many wealthy people ruining their lives with it? You see, the truly rich people will all tell you money is only important to a certain point. Once you have enough of it, it just doesn't matter anymore. It's not important. That's why if the only thing you have is wealth you can still be miserable.

People who have placed their hope in money have lived under the misconception that money buys happiness. When they finally get the money and they still aren't happy, then they begin trying all sorts of

Notes:

_____

_____

_____

_____

weird things in search of happiness. It's why so many famous and rich people ultimately sink their own ship. So, if money and fame aren't the answer to happiness, what is?

First, don't get me wrong; we should always strive to be financially free. Financial freedom can mean no bondage to creditors. The point is we don't have to be financially rich to be financially free. However, there's one more thing to add.

Along my journey, I was also developing a close "relationship," with God. Note I didn't say religion, rather a relationship. This relationship, in itself, is a lifelong journey that never ends. With each year of my life that passes, my relationship with God tends to grow stronger and deeper. Each time I begin to think I'm wise, I quickly realize there is much more to learn. I'm sure this will continue until the day I die.

Have you ever noticed that at each stage of life you sometimes think how ignorant you were at younger ages? At 21, I thought I was so mature. I would look back at those in high school (who thought they knew it all) and think of how immature they were. At 35, I couldn't believe how naive I was at 21. I think you get my point. The same seems to be true of my relationship with God. At each stage of my life, I would have times that I thought I had it all together. I felt in communion with God; family relationships were strong, and financially things were good. It would always seem about then, that I would learn another lesson in life.

Connie and I have two of the most beautiful children you can imagine. Inside and out, Kelly and Kris constantly bring us happiness as parents. They've made their mistakes and caused us grief at times, as any teenager or child would. But over-all, we couldn't imagine two children

Notes:

_____

_____

_____

_____

providing us with greater joy. Are our children this way because we were such awesome parents? No way! We did our best. However, the results are truly a blessing of God and He gets all the credit.

Whenever, our toughest times and lessons in life would surface, we would find ourselves looking for answers in the Bible. The closer our relationship with God would be, the more peace, joy and happiness we would find. Then, things may get going really good again, and suddenly, God was in the back seat. It was as if I was saying; "OK God, thanks for getting me this far, I can take it from here!" Then, after a time doing it my way, I would once again mess it all up and it was time to seek God again.

I have found God to be real and living and very much involved in my life. It's through this relationship that Connie and I have found true happiness. However, it comes from a source we seldom think of, our Creator.

Financial freedom can add to our family's happiness, being financially rich doesn't. In Philippians 4:12 & 13, Paul says; " *I know what it is to be in need and I know what it is to have plenty. I have learned the secret of being <u>content in any and every situation</u>, whether well fed or hungry, whether living in plenty or in want. I can do all things through Him who gives me strength.* " It is in this relationship with God that happiness is found. You can't take your wealth with you when you die. I heard it said once that I've never seen a Brinks truck following a hearse. I've also heard it said that money just shifts from one person to the next. As we journey through life, we accumulate money. Then when we die, the money is dispersed to others and the cycle starts all over again. However, no one ever really "owns" it.

Notes:

_____

_____

_____

_____

Are you trying to find happiness through obtaining more money? Read the magazines! Read about the lives of so many who do have the money. Are they truly the happiest people? Or, are those who have a relationship with their creator, those who have a relationship with family and those financially free the ones who are truly rich and successful in life.

In Mark 8:36 it says; *"What good is it for a man to gain the whole world, yet forfeit his soul?"* Are you spending all of your time trying to get more money? Take a look around you. You'll find more treasure than you could ever imagine, right within your own household, your own family, and a relationship with God.

I have found that my relationship with God comforts me in times of stress, worry, anxiety and fear. If you would like to know more about this relationship, I would like to recommend a few books.

For people newly seeking a relationship with God, I recommend:

"More Than A Carpenter" by Josh McDowell

If you would like to dig deeper, I would recommend the following titles:

"The Life You've Always Wanted"   **by John Ortberg**
"The God You're Looking For"   **by Bill Hybels**
"What Is The Father Like"   **by Phillip Keller**
"The Pursuit Of Holiness"   **by Jerry Bridges**

Always remember, the secret to success does not involve more money. True success involves what money can never buy. In God's eyes, you

Notes:

_____

_____

_____

_____

are more valuable than you could ever imagine. Once you realize your value to Him, you will know the secret to success in life.

I know the ideas presented in this book can provide you the tools to finding financial freedom. Now, it's up to you. Will you use them? While finding your financial freedom may take time, it will happen if you're patient.

The Living Bible says; *"But these things I plan wont happen right away. Slowly, steadily, surely, the time approaches when the vision will be fulfilled. If it seems slow, do not despair, for these things will surely come to pass. Just be patient! They will not be overdue by a single day"*.

Now, allow me to leave you with this prayer found in Colossians 1:11&12.

"We pray that you will be filled with his mighty, glorious strength so that you can keep going, no matter what happens – always full of the joy of the Lord, and always thankful to the Father, who has made us fit to share all the wonderful things that belong to those who live in the kingdom of light."

May God richly bless you and your family. May you find financial freedom and the **true** riches you seek.

Notes:

_____

_____

_____

_____

APPENDIX A

INVESTMENT OPTIONS

At FFEI, it is our goal to remain unbiased in our advice. However, we also realize that many of our clients are not sure of where to begin concerning their investment portfolio. If you have a financial planner, we recommend consulting them about what investments may best meet your needs. In the event you do not have an advisor, we have listed below several mutual fund companies that we are confident you would be able to work directly with to open your mutual fund.

Listing of the following fund families is not to be construed as a recommendation of these funds. There are many more that you may decide on through your own research. However, as a starting point, we have given some names and numbers you may decide to begin with.

AIM	800-959-4246
Alliance	800-227-4618
Fidelity	800-544-8888
Invesco	800-525-8085
MFS	800-637-2929
Oppenheimer	800-225-1581
Putnam	800-225-1581
Warburg Pincus	800-927-2874

If you invest on your own, each company would be happy to send you all of the information on each of their funds to help you make a good decision. You would want to be sure you only buy "C" shares, as there is no commission on these shares. As mentioned earlier, if you decide to use a financial advisor (recommended) then you would be buying "A" or "B" shares. While these come with commissions, the advice is almost always valuable.

APPENDIX B

CREATE ADDITIONAL CASH FLOW

*Creative ways for discovering & generating extra CASH FLOW....
working your way toward FINANCIAL FREEDOM*

POTENTIAL MONEY SAVERS	Estimated 1-Time Savings	Actual 1-Time Savings	Estimated Monthly Savings	Actual Monthly Savings	Willing to Do?
1. Sell items you have which you don't need. Have a garage sale, hop on E-Bay, etc.					
2. Donate items you couldn't sell (see tax write-off example)					
3. "Shop" your own closet-you may rediscover some hidden clothes you forgot about. (Or maybe they're back in style)					
4. Call around for insurance rates (auto, home, etc.) consolidate with one insurer.					
5. Get rid of PMI (private mortgage insurance) Check with mortgage company if you currently pay this.					
6. Refinance current Mortgage (see formula)					
7. Buy haircut scissors if you have several children (and can cut hair well enough to get by)					
8. Increase Tax Exemptions, if getting large yearly refunds.					

CREATE ADDITIONAL CASH FLOW

*Creative ways for discovering & generating extra CASH FLOW....
working your way toward FINANCIAL FREEDOM*

POTENTIAL MONEY SAVERS	Estimated 1-Time Savings	Actual 1-Time Savings	Estimated Monthly Savings	Actual Monthly Savings	Willing to Do?
9. Start packing a lunch instead of eating out.					
10. Cancel your newspaper or magazine subscriptions.					
11. Cancel your cable TV, or get rid of the movie channels.					
12. Clip some coupons...shop the sales.					
13. Join a warehouse club, and buy, cook in bulk.					
14. Auto scale back (sell the Jaguar, buy a ???) or rethink your current lease.					
OTHER IDEAS... GET CREATIVE!!!					
15. _____					
_____					
_____					
_____					
16. _____					
_____					
_____					
TOTAL AMOUNT TO BE USED TOWARD FINANCIAL FREEDOM					

APPENDIX C

MONTHLY BUDGET GUIDELINES

(Net) Household Income $ _____

Charity	10% = $ _____	Actual _____
		+/- $ _____
Investments	10% = $ _____	Actual _____
		+/- $ _____
Housing	29% = $ _____	Actual _____
		+/- $ _____
Utilities	4% = $ _____	Actual _____
		+/- $ _____
Food	10% = $ _____	Actual _____
		+/- $ _____
Rec/Entertainment	3% = $ _____	Actual _____
		+/- $ _____
Vacation	3% = $ _____	Actual _____
		+/- $ _____
Auto/Transportation	10% = $ _____	Actual _____
		+/- $ _____
Medical	1% = $ _____	Actual _____
		+/- $ _____
Telephone	2% = $ _____	Actual _____
		+/- $ _____
Clothing	4% = $ _____	Actual _____
		+/- $ _____
All Insurances	6% = $ _____	Actual _____
		+/- $ _____
Repair/Maint.	2.5% = $ _____	Actual _____
		+/- $ _____
Misc.	5.5% = $ _____	Actual _____
		+/- $ _____

APPENDIX D

PAYING CASH FOR A CAR
(NO DOWN PAYMENT)

1. Buy a $4,000 to $5,000 car.

2. Make payments of $350/mo. Car is free and clear in 12 months.

3. Continue payments to 6% interest investment for last 12 months.

4. At end of 2 years on first car, you have $6,317 for next car.
   - $4,317 saved
   - $2,000 for old car

5. Invest $375/mo. for next two years, pay $12,537 CASH for next car.
   - $9,573 saved
   - $3,000 for old car

6. Invest $400 per month for next two years, pay $16,173 CASH for next car.
   - $10,173 saved
   - $ 6,000 for old car

7. Invest $425 per month for next two years, pay $18,809 CASH for next car.

Paying Cash for a Car

1. Buy a $4,000 to $5,000 car for cash.
   (Equity in current car)

2. Save $350/mo. for 24 months

3. At end of 2 years on first car, you pay $10,901 CASH for next car.
   $8,901 saved
   $2,000 for old car

4. Save $375/mo. for 24 months, pay $14,937 CASH for next car.
   $9,537 saved
   $5,400 for old car

5. Invest $400/mo. for next two years, pay $17,673 CASH for next car.
   $10,173 saved
   $ 8,800 for old car

6. Invest $425 per month for next two years, pay $18,973 CASH for next car.